Chairbound

to

Heaven Bound

D1730422

Chairbound
to
Heaven Bound

Jean Neil

New Wine Press

New Wine Press

An imprint of
Roperpenberthy Publishing Ltd
Springfield House,
23 Oatlands Drive,
Weybridge,
Surrey
KT13 9LZ

ISBN 978-1-905991-76-1

Typeset by **documen**, www.documen.co.uk
Printed in the United Kingdom

CONTENTS

Foreword

The story of Jean Neil is heart-stirring and touching. She was a zero with a ONE in front. Jesus turned her into a ten, a Holy Spirit firebrand. What God does is marvellous in our eyes. I saw Jean Neil for the first time March 12th, 1988 at the National Exhibition Centre in Birmingham, UK. She had been brought desperately ill in a wheelchair, which her husband John pushed. When I entered the hall packed with 12,000 mostly young people I quietly started to pray, "Lord, what will you do tonight? Which key-miracle will you perform?" The Holy Spirit said to me, "The woman with the green dress in the wheelchair I will heal tonight". It was Jean. When I went to her I said, "Jesus will heal you tonight. I will pray for you and then you will stand up." Her husband John replied, "What do you mean 'stand up'? My wife has no hips." The glorious miracle happened anyway. Jean ran a marathon that night, full of strength and health. To read this happening in her own words is truly moving.

With her healing the Lord gave Jean a calling, a wonderful calling. She has crisscrossed the globe many times sharing, preaching, teaching and praying for the sick. She is a great example when it comes to faith in action. This book will inspire and bless anyone who reads it. I highly recommend it, and wish Jean and her family God's richest blessings.

Rev. Reinhard Bonnke, Evangelist

Preface

My first memory of Jean Neil was at the beginning of her ministry.

Jean was thrown in the deep end when in 1988 at a Pentecostal meeting Rev. George Canty told Jean to "Pray for that man." The man was head and shoulders taller than Jean. Undaunted, Jean reached out to lay hands on him where she could and he was immediately healed of a frozen shoulder. The next person was a woman who was having marital problems. As Jean prayed she saw the face of a man imposed on the woman. Jean revealed that she knew that she was also seeing someone. The next evening the woman walked in with her new partner and introduced him to Jean, who commented, "I met you last night". The man was surprised that she knew who he was.

In 1992, at an African style crusade held by C.F.A.N. in Perry Park, Birmingham, England, Reinhard Bonnke had asked Jean to minister. Jean rang me from Rugby requesting accommodation for a U.N. Diplomat from France and his wife, a nursing sister, who was suffering from kidney failure who wanted to attend the crusade.

On reaching the U.K. they rang me saying that his wife had lost the use of her legs when the line suddenly went dead! Concerned I contacted Jean who made enquiries and we found ourselves visiting a house in Perry Barr where this nursing sister now lay paralysed from the waist down and with kidney problems.

As Jean laid hands on the wife she received a divine word of knowledge. The nursing sister revealed that her parents had been missionaries in Africa and being incensed at being left on her own for months on end in a boarding school she had told the school children that she was an orphan.

Jean advised her to ask God's forgiveness for denying her parentage and as she responded she started to receive feeling back into her legs. She got out of bed and met her astonished host's wife at the top of the stairs where they embraced crying. Later at the crusade both her hosts gave their hearts to the Lord.

In this book "only the half can be told". I have worked alongside many healing evangelists and I believe Jean's strength comes from the amount of time she spends with each person and the sincerity with which she carries out her wonderful ministry.

Pastor Stan Taylor

1 *As a Baby*

The Island of Jersey is the largest of the Channel Islands, its capital being Saint Helier. The Island is divided into 12 Parishes. Each Parish is headed by a Constable who is elected for a four year period by the residents of the Parish. The Constable also represents the municipality in the states.

There is an Honorary Police force in each Parish. They have, for centuries, been selected by the parishioners to assist the Constable of the Parish to maintain law and order.

The Bailiff of Jersey is the chief justice of the Channel Islands. They serve as president of the legislature and have ceremonial and executive functions.

The Bailiffs and deputy Bailiffs are appointed by the Crown, not by the government or legislatures of the Islands and may hold office until retirement age, which is 70 in Jersey and 65 in Guernsey, which is the second largest of the Islands..

A duty Bailiff may preside in the Royal Court and the state Chamber when the Bailiff is not available.

Senior Jurats may be appointed as Lieutenant-Bailiffs to perform duties in lieu of the Bailiff on occasions, as well as presiding over judicial proceedings generally of an administrative nature.

The population was 158,000, when last I heard. The span of the island is 5 miles x 9 miles, which is 45 sq miles. It also has its own currency.

Jersey is a beautiful place where people come for holidays or for a honeymoon. Many rich people like film stars and millionaires buy property and live there to avoid paying tax, although they are charged a high tax at the beginning of their stay in Jersey. I may add that a film star called Lily Langtry, better known to the islanders as The Jersey Lily, is buried on the island.

Charlie Chaplin also lived in Jersey in 1912. Other well known people were Nigel Mansell and Derek Warwick, well-known racing drivers, golfer Ian Woosnam and journalist Alan Whicker, who is buried on the island. There were many more well known people of the era who also lived in Jersey.

The birch was used as a deterrent against crime. This would take place in the prison grounds with a doctor attending and the guilty person would have twelve lashes of the birch on their back, then they would have salt rubbed into the wounds. Only one man ever had the birch twice, the second time was for a stupid dare.

In 1940, during World War Two, the Germans came from France and occupied the Island. Times, it seems, were tough, what with regimental ruling, curfews and ration books.

Petrol was scarce at times and the only people that could have petrol were the doctors. Coal, tea and coffee were also very hard to get. In fact, at times there were none of these things in the shops. People would roast rose petals and blackberry leaves together to make coffee.

The Germans were always on the alert to find out if people had any form of radio, fearing anyone would make contact the mainland. It was customary for them to come and search the houses or hotels and even rip up the floorboards looking for these radios. No one dared cause a fuss about it as they would just kill you. They also would just put you out of your home and put their own men in to live there. This happened on a regular basis.

Underground tunnels were being dug out by the prisoners. One such tunnel being built but never finished was a place called The Underground Hospital. This is not a favourite of the Jersey people because we knew what it was really being built for. Prisoners that took sick or died whilst they were building the tunnel were thrown in with the building mixtures and plastered into the walls. Gas chambers were to be installed for such purposes for the sick and the elderly and even babies, as the story goes. It is a very dark cold dismal place and has now been made into a tourist attraction for visitors to visit.

French girls were brought from France for the Germans, as no Jersey girl would have a date with a German soldier, because if found out she would be tarred and feathered for the shame.

I do not recall much of the happenings of wartime, being a young child.

1945 was to see the war end and the liberation of Jersey which followed with much joy and partying.

Jersey is a beautiful holiday resort and has many places of beauty, and is full of historic places to visit, also the night life. In August every year there is the Battle of Flowers. This is a very colourful day when exhibits of various flowers are adorned and there is a big parade when the exhibits are judged. This, it seems, goes back years. People start the building of these exhibits in January. A Miss Battle of Flowers is chosen at a beauty parade during the year. People turn out in great crowds to see this procession, then in the evening there is a night of music and dancing.

The Island is well known for tax free products. Clothes, food and the general cost of living for the locals is very expensive, together with any medical treatment.

The Jersey cow is known for its rich milk and the cream which is sold in shops and markets. Jersey is well known for products such as potatoes, tomatoes, honey, fish, crabs and shellfish.

The Island also grows beautiful variations of flowers. These are packed in boxes and transported to people for gifts.

Jersey is well worth a holiday or honeymoon. If you have not been there yet, I would recommend you visit.

I was born in Jersey, Channel Islands on the 10th of July 1935 at the hospital into a family of eight girls, Edith, Nellie, Barbara, Joyce, Pauline, Monica and Roselle and three brothers William, Clifford and Richard. My mother, it seems, had a couple of miscarriages.

At a very early stage of my childhood, we were all taken away from my parents due to lack of proper parental care. Later in life, through searching my life history through the Jersey Archives and other means, I have learnt the truth about why we were put into children's homes. My father was always drunk and very cruel, especially to the boys, and would speak and do provocative things to the girls. They all had a real fear of him. When our mother heard dad coming home she would apparently call "up parliament" and everyone would hide. He was well known at his local, called the Don Inn. He took out his temper or the effects of his hangover on the family which, it seems, were most days.

The boys worked on a farm as they grew up and dad would take their wages off them for drink to suffice his drinking problem.

He beat the boys with his leather belt until they screamed with pain and they were bleeding. He even threatened to use the belt on the girls, when he came home drunk from the pub. In fact Richard was scarred for life down both arms to his fingers because the boys had been playing with matches and dad took him and held both his arms to the fire until they blistered.

My sister Roselle told me years later that mum could not be bothered to fetch me from my cot in the mornings. She would make the girls fetch me downstairs. They would say, "Jean is crying. She is in a mess". Mum would reply, "leave her to cry, it will not hurt her", but they would still fetch me and bring me downstairs and mum would get really angry with them. Roselle was only four years older than me, and if she fetched me from my cot she would pick me up and when she got to the stairs she would sit down and come down the stairs on her bottom.

What kind of mother is that, I ask myself? Was I a mistake? Was I really wanted? I felt the black sheep of the family.

One day the police were called because Clifford and William made a remark about dad coming home drunk again and he threw a metal instrument which almost cut Clifford's ear off completely and he needed hospital treatment. My dad also stabbed one of the uncles the same evening.

The police were called to the house and found me lying in the same cot as my sister Monica who had been dead for a few days. When the lady officer picked her out of the cot, not realising she was dead, her nightwear fell off her because she was so thin. She also lacked nutrition as we all did.

They went to school very often without any breakfast and were often having to hitch a lift on the milk cart to even get to school as they had missed the bus.

My father lodged at many different houses over the years and was known for his lust for women and I am sure if he was drunk he would not care which house he was staying the night in.

He always walked with a gait and would never walk on the pavement, always in the middle of the road. He had both his ankles broken, also his arm, as he was attacked and set upon because of his evil actions, which I would rather not go into.

I cannot honour my parents for what happened to me but I can honour them that they brought me into the world, also that I know that an American couple wanted to adopt me and my father would not sign the adoption papers.

Roselle remembers hiding behind the chair that night we were removed from our parents and remembers seeing all the blood on the floor. She said she was afraid dad would find her. She always said to me that there was a sister between her and me, and her name was Monica, so I have no doubt about all these happenings.

The police removed my mother and father and we were taken to the general hospital to be medically checked. In fact we were in there quite some time.

My sisters were taken to the Girls' Home. One brother went to Haut De La Garenne which was later in the news regarding all the abuse. I do not know where the other brothers went other than working on the farm.

After being released from the hospital I was taken to a children's home called the Westaway Crèche which was for ages from birth till the child was six years of age.

This orphanage was founded by Julia Westaway through a charity for poor children who gave £10 to the founding of the Crèche and £4,000 towards the maintenance. She left £80,000 to £90,000 to set up a charity to provide poor children with shoes. To this day most schools in Jersey have a cupboard full of gym shoes provided by Julia.

I was looked after well as far as I can recall. I do not remember being ill-treated during that time. I can recall certain things that happened such as having to go for daily walks with the nursery nurses wearing long dresses and raincoats down to our ankles, floppy rain hats and big wellington boots, probably too big for us we would be tied together to each other with a long strap, fearing one of us would stray. We would spend a lot of time on the beach as the nursery was close by. People would make comments like, "Oh, look at those little orphan kids. I wonder what happened to their parents". We were made to believe that we were orphans so we believed it. Another remark would be if one of us was having a tantrum and screaming. "Look at the behaviour of that child. If she were my kid I would tan that kid's backside with a slipper." I would just put my tongue out at them and grin. Smacking children was legal in those days and I am sure I had a few smacks in my life. It did not do us any harm as we needed to be taught right from wrong whilst we were still learning.

I can still remember playing in a red tin car racing up and down the playground, also pedalling an old three wheeler bike where the pedals kept falling off because the bike was so old and rusty.

These memories have stayed in my mind all these years.

I grew up to be a rebel, and it seems I was one even in those early years of my life and was often the one to start doing the mischief and upsetting the other children.

We never knew what it was like to have our own toys. Even the toys we played with in the playground did not belong to any individual. We had to share them with everyone. They would be toys given to the nursery from other people. At Christmas I would have a doll or teddy bear but even that was second-hand. I remember one Christmas when I was about four years of age, poor old Father Christmas got too close to the candles on the tree and his beard caught fire and they threw buckets of water over him to put the flames out. It was frightening yet funny when he was all wet.

I had very curly hair as a child and still have to this day. We all had to do a party piece on Christmas day and the nurse taught me to sing On the Good Ship Lollipop which was a favourite of Shirley Temple who was a film star. This was always a special day for us.

During the six years I never saw any one of my family, as I recall. There was no one out there other than the nurses that looked after me. I missed out on the natural cuddles from my mum and dad and growing up with my siblings. This, I suppose to me, was the norm, but now I look back and realise how important mothers and fathers, brothers and sisters as a family are, to be able to have that special time growing up and bonding with them all and doing the things together that a normal family would do. The matron was a Mrs Le Quesne and the sister was Miss Hall, another sister Nora Farrow, and kindergarten teacher Alice Hall. These people were kind to us and looked after us as best they could. They were there for me unlike my parents who forgot, I am sure, that I existed. There were many false accusations that the children in the Crèche had German fathers but that was not true and I can assure you that my father was not a German. He was a true Jersey man.

You can choose your friends; you cannot choose your family. The first years of a child's life are the most important where the parents are directly responsible for the effect and personality of the child for the rest of their life. Make sure you give your children the best upbringing you can. They are your responsibility and, most of all, they rely on you.

I never had the experience of sitting on my parents' knees and having that special kiss and a cuddle from them or even being told that they loved me. Often, even now, I wonder what it would have been like to experience something like that. Even in the Bible, Jesus took the little children and blessed them. Matthew's Gospel chapter 19 verse 14.

From this experience of what I missed in those first six years and also through my teens I learnt to hopefully never make the same mistake with my own children, if I had any, as this is so important. As a child is growing up, the discipline is needed but the love is very important.

I still have a very vivid picture of that nursery. It is now used to house doctors and nurses but when I go back to visit Jersey I stand and look at that building. That is where I was raised as a child until I was six years of age. It will always have those memories of where I lived.

2 *Abuse and Suffering*

||||||||||||||||||||||||||||||||||||||||||||||||||||||||||||||||||||||||||||||||||||||||||||||||||||||||||||||||

When I was six years of age, I was taken to the matron who told me and that I was going to a party at a big house where there would be lots of other girls. That part was true but there was to be no party. I was given a brown suitcase, with all my belongings packed inside, put in a car and driven to this big house and handed over to this lady. I heard a lot of noise and really believed there was a party. What a lie that was. I did not envisage what I was going to face over the following nine years of my young life. It reminds me now of the film Annie, which I can never watch as it is too close to reality of what happened all those years back.

I was taken to a girl who was four years older than I was and was told she would be looking after me. She said, "my name is Roselle". I said, "my name is Jean". I was surprised to find out later that I was one of a large family and she was in fact my sister, but another shock was to find I had more sisters and also some brothers, also a mother and father. I was puzzled and started asking questions. I wanted to know why I was not with them before this. Why did my mother and father give me to those other people to be looked after? Why have I only just found out that I had such a large family, but they were complete strangers to me? I could not say Roselle, so I called her my big sister, but what is a sister, I thought? What was she going to do with me as she was a complete stranger? I had left all my friends at the other home and now I have to start all over again meeting new people.

I was told that we were taken away and separated because my father had a drinking problem and would get quite violent at times and that my mother had a hard life with my father and his drink problem. I was angry and resentful as I missed out on so much, not knowing that I had any family and being frowned upon as an orphan. I experienced hatred, bitterness and resentment even at that young age. This I held for many years. It was only later in my life that I found out the real truth of what really happened. I would cry a lot in bed at night as I did not know what the next few years would be like. Would these people be nice or horrible to me? To be with all these girls was frightening. It really was a battle for me with new girls, new staff and new rules. How would I cope?

My sister Roselle was there to look after me and tell me what to do and she confirmed that some of the other girls were in fact my sisters. In fact I really did not get to know them as they were so much older than I was and complete strangers to me. I was soon to find out that it was so different from the place I had been in. This one was like a prison the people were very strict. I was warned not to wet the bed or in the morning I would be taken down into the cellar where the staff would rub the wet sheet over my face and hair then beat me with stinging nettles on my bare skin. I remember shaking with fear because there was the odd occasion I would wet the bed and did not want to go to sleep that night in case that happened. I thought that they were supposed to be kind to us not hurt us but as the years went by I realised how wrong I was.

I remember the first night I wet the bed I got up early the next morning and hid my sheet under the mattress thinking they would not find it. They found the wet sheet and just as the girls had told me we were taken down into the cellar and had the sheet rubbed in our faces then were beaten with fresh nettles. We certainly did not smell very pleasant, and then the staff had to train us not to wet the bed. We were made to go to bed without a nightdress and nettles were put in the bed to remind us to get out of bed and go to the toilet. I must say I always remembered that cellar after a few times of being down in it. The cellar was also used as a place where the staff would beat us with a wooden hairbrush or a cane and you tried not to cry or they beat you again to give you something to cry for. To stop us screaming because of the pain a gag was put across our mouth to muffle the screams. At night, when put to bed, it was a regular pattern for a couple of the girls to be given something to make them sleepy then be taken downstairs into a room where the staff met at night with male friends, and what happened with us only God knew as I am positive we were drugged for the pleasures of the staff and their male friends. We were too afraid to say anything to anyone, even at school, as the headmaster was part of it. One set of clothing per week, the other set in the wash, not good if you soiled the underwear and clothes.

As time went by I got a bit bolder and started answering back, to which they would give you a slap across the face or hit you with whatever they had in their hand, even a wooden hairbrush. All you could do was try and duck away from them. When you wanted toilet paper, you would have to find one of the staff and ask for it. The big girls got two pieces the smaller girls had one piece. When we asked why the bigger girls had two pieces we were told it was because they had bigger bottoms. Too bad if you had a problem such as an upset stomach. The food we had was disgusting and only fit to give to the pigs.

Each girl had set jobs to do each day and those were checked to see if they were done properly. Punishments were dished out on a regular basis, such as doing the potatoes for a week for all the girls and the staff, and you could only use cold water. The staff that was on potato shift would come to check every potato was to her satisfaction and if it was not we went to the matron's sitting room and had the cane. I remember starting a fight with another girl who was always calling me names, and because of this I would have to be punished. The punishments that were dished out to us were very hard, bearing in mind we were not very old and whoever was on duty stood over you making sure the job was done properly. If not, she made you start from the beginning. On that occasion I was taken to the kitchen and told my punishment was to get on my hands and knees and scrub the whole floor. The tiles had raised bubbles on them so if by any chance you would wash one part and scrub the next bit, obviously when it dried you saw the difference, so whoever was in charge of that duty would stand over you and pick up the pail of dirty water and throw it over the floor and you had to start again. Ice cold baths of water would be another way of punishment where the staff would put you in the bath of cold water with ice in the bath, throw you in and hold your head under the water until you gasped for breath. This would happen on a daily basis to girls, then they would beat you with a cane.

Carbolic soap was used to wash our mouths out if anyone used bad language. Saturday seemed to be the highlight for the staff as there would always be a time of public beatings in front of all the other girls. Black points were given for bad behaviour. The three girls in each age group that had the most marks against their name would be stripped of all their clothing bent over a chair and beaten with a cane on the bottom. Once again you tried not to cry, yet what could you do, because that cane really hurt on your bare skin? I did experience this on several occasions. We were sent to our dormitory where we would lie on the bed with our face pressed into the pillow to muffle the sound of the sobbing.

People have asked why we did not go to the authorities and tell them, but we were told people would not believe us as we were telling lies, and also the matron was a white witch and she always carried a large pair of scissors on her belt, and she would threaten us if we told anyone she would have our tongues cut out for telling lies. Can you imagine how frightened we were? We only had one pair of knickers which we wore for the whole week. We had one hanky for the week and on Sunday morning we all lined up in numerical order. I was number seven. In fact all our clothes were marked with our numbers on them. There was one of the staff holding a basket; in would go your dirty hanky and she would give you a clean one. No hanky, no breakfast until you found it. Hand me down clothes were the norm, no new clothes. Even pairs of shoes were handed down. If there were no shoes that fitted your feet, you went to school with bare feet, even in the winter. These situation stay in your mind and you do not forget them easily.

We went to a mixed school. The name was Grouville School and because we were dressed different to the other kids they called us horrible names, and being bullied was not nice. I was a gang leader and so I was always at the headmaster's study for fighting with other children as I would stand up for myself. I enjoyed school on the whole and even passed the grade for college but obviously being in the home that was a no go. We missed out on lots of things due to our situation of being in the home. On the way home from school, if we were seen fighting with a boy or rolling about on the ground and one of the staff passed by in her car, we would be called to the sick room and examined by a so called doctor friend of the home, followed by a sponge brush dipped in neat disinfectant to clean us out for fear that we might have had sex with that boy. The pain and the stinging of the disinfectant made you scream. It was almost done for the pleasure of the staff as some of them were lesbians. We did not know what sex was anyway, so in our minds we thought that if you touched a boy or rolled on the ground with him you got pregnant. We were completely innocent and I suppose naive as we knew nothing about these things. They were alien to us. I certainly had made up my mind, if anyone was nasty to me I was going to always make sure I stood up for myself and would fight my own battles. If anyone dare come against me they got what they were asking for, no matter what the punishment I got afterwards. In that type of environment you do not let people walk all over you or your life would be so miserable and you would be looking over your shoulder the whole time.

Friday was always special for those of us who were chosen to be in the choir in the church. I was in the choir and we would go for a practice. The organist was the vicar's wife. When the practice was over, and because we were hungry, it was over the vicar's garden wall to go stealing his apples. The vicar's dog would bark and the vicar would chase us. It seemed it was his duty to phone the matron and she would be waiting to meet us on the homeward journey, hence a good beating with the cane. Harvest Thanksgiving was always tempting in church as we never saw fruit at the home. The girls who sat in the front seats would pass some of the fruit to the girls at the back. At this point the vicar would stop the service and chant a prayer asking God to forgive us for stealing the fruit because his wife had seen us doing it through her mirror and she would then send a message to her husband. Obviously we were punished for stealing the fruit. Everybody went to church on Sunday morning, all in a long line in twos. We would walk to the church which was a short way from the home. On special services we would be given one penny to put in the offering bag. Drop your penny and it cost you your Sunday dinner. One girl actually went without her Christmas dinner because she dropped her offering on the floor.

I remember one Sunday service the vicar said something that was wrong and five of us in the front pew laughed so much that we wet ourselves and there were puddles on the floor. We got up at the end of the service and walked home in our wet knickers as if nothing had happened. During the lunch break the matron announced that the vicar was upset because we had wet his floor. The five of us had to walk to the church with mop and bucket to wash the floor then back to the home for a thrashing with the cane. Night times were frightening. If anyone was caught talking after lights went out or was caught getting out of bed you were marched down the long corridor and made to stand for hours on cold wooden floors with nothing on your feet. You dare not sit down if you got tired. You would get a good smack across the head and face and made to stand there even longer.

We did learn various trades in the home. I know from that experience how it helped me in later years. There were sewing and knitting classes, cookery and arts and crafts. Fun was what we invented, which often got us into trouble more than we needed to, but there was never much to do. As time went by the more rebellious I was. At the age of fourteen I organised with nine other girls to run away from the home. The day and time had to be planned, which it was. Obviously we had to put on different clothes and we stole the staff's make-up to make us look older and off we went. We ran and ran so fast we were panting and puffing away as the first part was all uphill. I organised what we would do and where we would eat, even if it meant stealing or finding out where some of the girls' families lived and they would feed us and sleep us for the night. We spoke to the police most days, obviously not being seen altogether. That would be too obvious, and it went on for ten days. It was fun whilst it lasted.

I thought it was time we gave ourselves up so we went to the police and said we wanted to go back to the home. We were left on our own in the foyer whilst the police went to fetch our transport which was a big black van named The Black Maria. When they returned we had done a runner and the police caught up with us in the town and frogmarched us back to the police station with one arm behind our back. The police asked who the ringleader was and my friends pointed at me, so I decided to come clean and own up. The girls were taken back to the home where they were beaten with the cane and put into the ice cold bath of water. I was put into a cell for the night to answer questions about where we had slept and eaten. They were not amused to hear me tell them that we had spoken to them most days and laughed at the poster that was in the town asking people to look out for us. The follow day I was taken back to the home and had the normal punishment plus two weeks on dry bread and water and had to sleep on the bare wooden floor, no mattress or blanket, not even a sheet to cover me. When I wanted the toilet I had to ring the buzzer and the staff escorted me there and back. At the end of the first week I was told if I said sorry they would let me off the second week of punishment. I told them I was not doing that. I was a gang leader and I would have had to face the humiliation from the rest of my gang for giving into the staff, so I had the next week as well.

Saturdays we had to do exercises in the garden, which was jumping up and down and putting your arms in the air as you did the first lap around the garden. The second time round we had to put our hands to our sides, and then put them out whilst jumping up and down. All we wore was our pants, even in the winter. When the apples were on the trees that was fun, as we would grab the apples from the trees and stuff them in our pants. At the end of the exercises the person in charge would get us all in a line and ask for all the apples we had picked, telling us that the gardener would be pleased with us helping him do his job. We would get out of the bedroom windows at night, slide down the drainpipe, get some apples in a pillowcase and climb back up the pipe, only to find the matron standing at the window waiting for us because one of the girls had split on us. The result was a good beating for stealing. To frighten the staff we would climb up on the eaves of the roof of the high building and refuse to come down, so they would call the fire brigade to fetch us down. When they arrived we would shin back down the pipes and stand with the other girls looking all innocent. I suppose at times we deserved the punishment we got.

3 *Changing Homes*

After all the things I went through in the home, I thought there has got to be more to life than this. Coming to the age of fifteen, I am told I was being prepared for service, which meant working on a farm and living with a family, but would still be under the rules of the home. By this time all my sisters had left the home and worked for other people. I did learn that Pauline and Joyce worked for a doctor as nannies to their children, and Roselle went to work for the people who registered births and deaths. I lost all trace of them in spite of Jersey being so small. I do not know what happened to the others sisters. I never saw my brothers. I was on my own again.

The day came for me to leave the home and all my friends, which I found upsetting, having to say goodbye and move to another house. I had lived with these girls who had become my friends. I did not miss my sisters or my brothers, as when they left the homes I never saw them. I thought to myself this has got to be better than being beaten and sexually abused all the time. I was told I would be living with a Jewish family and to behave myself, otherwise I would be back at the home for punishment, and told I was still under the home's ruling and still under the responsibility of the county court and the prison authorities, due to what my parents had done in the past. I lived for eighteen years imprisoned, bearing the burden of what my parents had done all those years back.

The people I was going to came to fetch me in the car. They seemed nice enough and gave me a big smile then shook my hand. They introduced themselves as Mr and Mrs Raphael. I got into the car with the few belongings that I had and I waved goodbye to my friends with tears running down my cheeks, took a hanky from my pocket, wiped the tears from my eyes, then I was driven away from the awful home that I had been in for nine years. I had hoped life was going to be happier living with a nice family. Arriving at the house it was so strange and I felt lonely without all my friends.

When we got to the house, which was quite large with a big garden in the front, I was soon to find out that it was a big farmhouse with cows, chickens, ducks, pigs and goats. That certainly made me think would I be looking after the animals. I was shown to my bedroom which was in the attic. It was clean and neat and had nice flowery wallpaper. Never having had my own bedroom, because there were always eight girls sharing the same dormitory, I thought it was very nice to have my own private room. I was given certain rules which I thought, here we go again, rules, rules and more rules which by the way were quite strict. The family invited me to have tea with them so they could get to know me and tell me about the chores I would be doing on a daily basis. The food was a treat and I really enjoyed the taste of good food which we seldom had in the girls' home. I had an early night as I was exhausted with all that went on that day and slept well.

The following morning, up at the crack of dawn, I was taken down to where the animals were and shown what the programme was before breakfast. This boy got a stool for me to sit on so that I could learn how to milk the cows by hand, as milking machines were not used in those days. I sat looking at the cow not knowing how to pull the teats to get the milk. It was strange learning what to do and what not to do. I soon got the gist of it as the week went by. The chickens had to be fed and cleaned out twice a week, which wasn't too bad, then it was the pigs that had to be fed and cleaned out. The smell was absolutely awful. It really put me off bacon for some time, especially when you see what they ate and the mud they wallowed in. I hated that job. Last but not least, it was the goats that had to be fed. One of the goats chased me every morning. I got fed up at times milking the cows by hand, and if I was in a bad mood I would kick the bucket of milk over and blame the cow. At the end of the day it was my word against the cow's, as the cow could not speak. When I had finished cleaning out the animals and feeding them, it was then time to have a wash or bath and have my well earned breakfast which I had to prepare for myself before getting ready for the house chores.

When I look back, I suppose all the cooking, cleaning, washing and sewing that we were taught to do was great because I knew what to do most of the time. I was still afraid sometimes in case I did something wrong. When you go through childhood looking over your shoulder and being afraid of everyone, you do not know what to expect. Having to call the lady of the house madam and her husband sir was strange to say the least, yet I did what they told me to do for fear of having to go back to the girls' home. They were fairly strict and I had to stay in my own quarters. The house was hard to keep clean, also they would have lots of friends that they would entertain until late at night and, of course, I had to look after the food and clearing each course of food, then all the washing up by hand, getting to bed late and still having to be up early next morning to do my chores on the farm.

I had very small wages from them, being told that they took my board and food into consideration. In all I was a slave to them at their beck and call at all times without grumbling. The good part was if I did grumble a bit there wasn't the fear of the cane or cold bath to follow. Every Wednesday afternoon I was allowed to have the time free from 2pm until 9pm, but what was I going to do? There was nowhere to go other than roam around town or go to the pictures and see a film with the small wage I got. Allowing me out, I had to promise to be back sharp at 9pm or I would lose that afternoon free the following week. They gave me an old rickety bicycle which rattled when I was riding it, because it was too far for me to walk into town and back. I did not have contact with my brothers or sisters, as I did not know where they were, and I certainly was not going to visit my mother or my father as I wanted nothing to with them after what I had been through. I somehow made contact with a couple of the girls who left the home around the same time as I did so we would spend the time together. At half past eight I would start the journey back to the house. On the way I had to pass a farm that had a great big dog. It would hear me coming along the road, wait for me to come close to the gate, then it would chase me up the road. I would peddle as fast as I could but the dog always knocked me off the bike so I got wise to this dog coming out and chasing me. I would get near to that farm, get off the bike, pick it up and carry it so the dog did not know I was going past and it worked every time.

After the first year it got really boring with those people and I missed seeing all my old friends in the home, so I decided to misbehave and give them lip and answer them back, then I could go back for a week to see my friends. Back to the home I went for a week, took my punishment like a soldier and had a great time sharing with the girls what it was like on the farm, and what the people were like. The time came for me to go back to the family. I must confess that I was sorry for what had happened because they treated me well, even though the work was hard.

As the next two years went by, I settled into a good routine making sure there was time to have a rest in case there were visitors coming for a meal, which meant a very late night. These became more regular as the time went on. One thing, they never made me or asked me to go to church, which I was not bothered about, because I had spent enough time in church. We had to go, whether we wanted to or not. We had no choice, so I was content not to go. In fact I had said that once I was older I would never go to church because it was boring. That idea changed a few years later and now I love being in church. I look back and wonder why. I thank God that He has had His hand upon my life right from my mother's womb. He was with me, I am sure, even though I did not realize it. Life is like going through a dark tunnel with struggles and strife, yet as we are going through the tunnel we are learning things all the time and I am sure the darkest part of the tunnel was in the home, then going to live with a family, and beginning to live a more normal life, that was another stage of the tunnel I had to come through and there were many more difficult situations that I would have to face in life as, at the age of eighteen, a choice had to be made whether to stay where I was on the farm or spread my wings like a baby bird leaves its mother and has to fend for itself. Although things were fairly good for me at that time, I really did not want to be cleaning out animals and feeding them all my life, so I decided I wanted more out of life and not being in a regimented atmosphere any longer, because that was what it was. Do this, do that, go here, go there. I had enough of that for all those years, once again thinking there must be more to life than being a slave to other people. I did not leave the farm straight away, as I had to decide where I wanted to go and what I wanted to do and what I wanted out of life. The people talked with me at great length about being out in the big wide world on my own and making sure I had accommodation. I said, "I am a fighter and will fight my way through life".

I applied to the hospital to see if they would accept me to do my nurse's training because I really wanted to help people. Getting the response that I had been accepted was great news. Also I knew that I would have somewhere to live and would not have to be looking for my own place. At the age of eighteen (whoopee) I was free at last from the court and prison authorities. Gone were the threats if I misbehaved of being taken back to the home of torture. I was told I was always welcome back to visit the family. I must confess that was not on my agenda. The past was the past. This was going to be a new beginning for me and no looking back. The day came for me to leave the farm and the family. It was sad leaving in one way, but hey I was going on the next stage of my life through the tunnel, obviously not knowing what life would be like for me. I said my tearful goodbyes and left the farm behind me, another chapter in my life that I really wanted to forget. Thinking back now, the right choice was made. My desire was to give hope and love to others that I had never ever experienced myself.

I really believed and felt things would get better as time went on. I could forget the years of cruelty, pain and suffering the sex abuse from the staff. How wrong I was, as later on in my life it all came back to reality when there was to be an investigation into the abuse that took place at Haut de la Garenne, which was where there were accusations of abuse and cruelty to the boys and the girls that had moved from the girls' home in Grouville and transferred to where the boys' home was. There were big articles in the newspapers, gruesome pictures shown on the television, and it all came flooding back. Do you ever forget horrible things that happened to you as a child? You do not talk about those things, but you learn to suppress it as if it never happened. Sooner or later, and at the right time, you have to release it and let it go, and that is why I have written this book, hoping it can be a help to those people who have gone through the same experiences. There are professional people who can counsel you to talk things over and to help you through the trauma of the past. I have had such counselling myself and found it very helpful to be able to talk and release the pent-up feelings that you have carried all those years.

4 *Nursing*

At the age of eighteen, once again facing the outside world on my own, I would have to make new friends in the nursing school. I was not afraid of the discipline as I had lots of practice in that area. I enjoyed the study work and got a good grade. I was having to borrow study books as I could not afford them at the time, and there was a limited time that you had to study from them, so I did a lot of overtime studying in my room. The day came to go onto the wards and put into practice what I had learnt. I felt a great relief that at last I was not just a slave to anyone but I was helping other people and have always known that, in spite of my past, there was a strong feeling of compassion for others, which helped me tremendously to understand the pain and suffering the patients were going through. I made friends with the other student nurses, which in fact has never been a problem for me at all, because I seemed to get on well with most people. My nursing career only lasted nine months, as I was taken seriously ill and collapsed unconscious on the floor when my appendix burst and I had peritonitis. Looking back I suffered a lot of pain in my stomach but took no notice of it, as I was used to pain with all the beatings as a child. The operation was done and my appendix removed. I then had a very bad infection that would not heal up. The doctor told me that due to the time I had spent in Intensive Care, and with so much weight loss, he felt it would be wise to take a lighter job. This really upset me but I took his advice and left nursing.

The next desire other than nursing was to help children who had a bad start in life like I did, so I applied for a position at the Westaway Crèche which was the children's home where I was as a baby, at which I was accepted. Of course I had to do the period of childcare training, whilst helping to look after the babies and the other children. I passed my exams and became a qualified nursery nurse. The compassion and feeling I had for those little ones was real, having been through that experience myself and knowing what those children were going to face in life until they were fifteen years of age, my heart went out to them. You understand more when you have experienced something personally. The thrill as I bathed, dressed and fed those babies was so special. To think that after all the abuse I had I could give so much love and even cuddle these children. When and if the children's parents came I would be so angry with them, knowing what the children were going to have to go through at the next homes. It was like they were oblivious to even giving it a thought. One mother had fifteen children. She would say it was her contribution to society. The strange thing was she had all boys. We would say she had her own football team plus the manager together with the linesmen.

We would take the bigger children for daily walks and also in the summer we spent mornings and afternoons on the beach, which was very near to the home. The children loved it on the sands and paddling in the sea. I would often take the group I was in charge of and buy them some sweets or an ice cream. Watching them playing with the toys that were similar to the ones we played with brought a lump to my throat. It was not easy having to relive those early years of my childhood. The memories came flooding back. My day off consisted of shopping or going to the pictures and by this time going out with boys, but I was always very cautious of them, thinking if they started giving me kisses and beginning to get too flirty and perhaps wanting more than that, I sorted them out by taking them for a walk by the harbour to see the big ships, then pushed them in the harbour and ran for dear life. This was because of the reaction from the staff at the girls' home when we had fights with the boys and they checked us to see if we had done anything to them.

There were many Italians working in the hotels in Jersey and, of course, some of the girls wanted to have a date with some of them but were too shy to ask them, so we would sort out a blind date for them. Margaret wanted such a date, so arrangements were made for her to meet one of the waiters from the Grand Hotel. A short distance from the hotel was a park where young lovers met. Margaret met André and they sat on a bench on the sea front and chattered for a while until he decided to go to the park. André was a bit hot blooded and he could not speak or understand English neither could Margaret speak or understand Italian. André started messing and trying to get her clothes off and she shouted, "I'll scream". He thought she wanted an ice cream so he took her to the hotel and got her an ice cream. This happened a second time and off to the hotel for a second ice cream, back up to the park with Margaret holding an ice cream in each hand and André holding onto her in case she ran off. Back to the park, André tells her he wants to make passionate love to her, as he is pulling at her clothes. Again she shouts "I'll scream". He says to her, " one ice cream okay, two ice creams okay, but three, you a pig" and slaps the ice cream in her face. She comes home crying and tells us what happened. André goes to work next day and tells his mates what happened so they had to explain to him that she did not want ice cream but that she was going to scream to get help, which I am sure his mates had a good laugh at, like we did. Another girl wanted a date with an Italian chef. She was very sure of herself and thought she knew what to do and say. She had learnt how to say sporcaccione, which in English means dirty man, but she did not know that so we primed her what to do when she met her chef. She was to go up to him and he would ask if she could speak the language. Obviously she said yes, and he wanted to know what she knew. She was to make amorous eyes at him and pucker her lips in a gesture she wanted to kiss him, then say the Italian word that she knew. She did as we had primed her, and he gave her a good slap and walked away, hence she was not keen on dating any Italian after that. I never met up with any of my siblings or visited my parents as I had no interest at the time in meeting up with them. The folk I worked with were my friends.

The sister in charge of us at the nursery was a Christian. Her name was Gaye Bastin. She would tell me all the time that I needed Jesus in my life. Considering we were forced to go to church in the Girls' Home, no way was I going to go to church when I was older. She would tell me the difference between giving your heart to Jesus and going to heaven when you die or turning away from Jesus and going to hell. I would laugh at her and say that I did not care where I went when I died. She said, "I am going to pray for you every morning and every evening until God answers my prayer because, Jean, you are such a rebel and you need be changed". That lady prayed as she said she would and many times I would mock her that God had not answered her prayers. Perhaps God did not really want me in heaven with Him. Gaye gave me invitations to go to a meeting with her, just to see what I thought. A change of shift duty was the answer for me at the time, but I realised that you cannot run away from God all the time. She kept praying and I kept running calling her a Bible basher and other names. She never gave up on me and neither did God. She went to a Brethren Church. They often had special meetings and they were having a special weekend to celebrate Easter. I was invited to the meeting on Good Friday and she assured me if I went and did not like it she would leave me alone and just pray for me each day for God to do something in my life. I was 19 years of age at the time.

I decided that I would go and take nine other nurses with me and we would play around during the meeting so they would throw us out. Into this little hall we went, laughing our heads off. We were chastised and told to behave as we were in church. We had got a plan to disrupt the meeting. We were to sing pop songs instead of the hymns, tell jokes and whilst the preacher was speaking we were going to chew bubble gum and blow bubbles so that they made a noise. The only seats left were ten in the front row. I was the leader of the gang but soon found out that doing things against God does not work because I could not think of one pop song to sing, neither could I remember any jokes, but you do not need brains to chew bubble gum and blow bubbles. The problem with that was they burst over our mouths and faces, which we then had to remove. I soon realised that when you try to do things against God it does not work and all of my planning went straight out of the window, as the saying goes. The speaker that night was Cyril Hocking from Wales. The minister introduced him and after he had greeted us he began to preach. He started by saying that he was going to tell us about a man called Jesus who died on a cross for everyone, even for rebels, and looked straight at us. I thought, the cheek of the man, and I told the girls it was all rubbish and we would run out of the church shouting "what a load of rubbish". When the time came to get off my chair I could not move, so had to stay and listen to the story. I had heard the Easter story many times, yet this was different. The preacher was stressing how God gave His son Jesus to die for our sins and how Jesus was accused for something He did not do. For the first time I really began to understand about the Cross, but I am thinking, which father, if he loved his only child, would let him be nailed on a cross, beaten and spat upon and ridiculed in front of everyone? I was not a very nice person, having so much hatred, resentment and bitterness in me, but my father would not have watched me die on a cross for the sins of others. There is not one of us that could ask any one of our children to give their lives to die in such a painful way to save the world.

As the story unfolded that night, I began to realise that Jesus died on that cross and took the pain of the nails in His hands and His feet, plus the beatings, together with the crown of thorns, for me, that I would not go to hell when I died but there would be a place in heaven for me. We started singing a hymn, The Old Rugged Cross, and the tears began flowing down my face. I could not control myself. I was feeling full of shame and remorse for the things I had done to other people. When the preacher started quoting John's gospel chapter 3 verse 16 "For God so loved the world that He gave His only son, that whosoever believed in Him would not perish but have everlasting life", I was still crying. He called people to the front who wanted to give their lives to Jesus. I was the first out of my seat and fell on my knees and four of my friends followed me. It was as if a great load had been lifted from me as I dedicated my life to Jesus. Miss Bastin, who had prayed for this day for a whole year, came and gave me a big hug. Her prayers had been answered. My heart changed that night from a heart of hatred to a heart of love and compassion towards others. Never give up on praying for your friends and family to get saved, because God never gave up on you. Joining that church was difficult as they were strict with what they believed in and really did what the Bible said. We wore hats, long dresses, could not wear any brooches, necklaces or makeup, and if we went without a hat there were always lots of head scarves for us to use and the women had to keep silent in the church. I must confess we were grounded on the Word of God. I was baptised by immersion in water, symbolising and showing to the world I had made a commitment to God. I did not fully understand it all, but a few years later got baptised again when I understood the true meaning of what I was doing and what it meant to die to the world and live my life for Jesus. Three hundred people attended that service with many giving their lives to Jesus.

5 *The Future*

I continued caring for the children over the next few years but at the age of twenty one I still did not have a steady boyfriend. Okay, there were lots of holiday makers that we went out with, but I wanted to look to settling down with a fellow. I found this magazine in the church which had come all the way from a church in Rugby in the United Kingdom. It had ten boys' names in it and they were looking for a pen friend so we thought they must be Christians like us. I got a pin from the lapel of my jacket and we had to shut our eyes and pick a name. I picked the name of this boy, John Neil. I wrote to John, then he wrote back to me and this went on for at least two years. I got a phone call from John saying he would like to visit me in Jersey to get to know me better. The day was arranged for me to meet him at the harbour off the night boat (John always had a fear of flying). As our eyes met I knew he was the one for me. He was really handsome and very polite. He made regular visits to see me and said he liked me very much and I made several visits to Rugby to meet his family. John did not have a happy childhood, as he was only ten when his father fell from his bike and was killed, so being the eldest of the children he became the man of the house. His mother was not always easy to get on with as she had mood swings. John eventually went to live with his uncle Jim Wooding and his granny who was quite a character at times.

The first time I visited Rugby I stayed at the Carlton Hotel. In those days you did not live together until you were married, not like it is today. I learnt some of Rugby's history on my visits, such as how the Rugby football game originated in Rugby after a boy at the Rugby School picked the ball up, ran with it and kicked it into the goal. A book called Tom Brown's School Days was written all about it. I also learnt that Guy Fawkes actually lived near Rugby in a village called Dunchurch, and the house he lived in was called Guy Fawkes' House. It was very expensive to come to Rugby so when it was my turn to come to see John I thought there has got to be a cheaper way than spending all this money to see John and have a kiss and a cuddle, so I called John on the phone and told him I could not afford to travel all the time as the pay I got was not good. If we got married it would be cheaper and John accepted this would be the best thing to do. The next visit we started making plans for our big day.

There were questions to be sorted out whether the wedding took place in Jersey or Rugby, which church, the best man, who would give me away, the bridesmaids and where the reception would take place. We decided that as I was going to leave Jersey the wedding would be in Jersey. This took about a year to sort everything out for the big day. My father heard I was getting married and asked me if he was giving me away. I told him no way was he having that honour because he gave me away as a baby and he was not going to give me away twice, and I told him to drop dead. My parents were not invited to the wedding. They had never done anything for me all those years back. I had been through my childhood and teenage years without them. I could do without them on my wedding day. I asked my brother William and he said he would give me away. His daughter Celia, my niece Margaret, and the pastor's daughter Ruth, were my bridesmaids.

John chose his best friend John to be best man, but it was not to be because John had an acid canister blow up in his face, so John asked his uncle Jim to step into John's place. The day we chose was March the third 1958 in Halket Place Church. The church I attended was too small. The reception was at my sister Pauline's mother in law's house. This was a strange time for me. I was getting married to leave my place of birth to go to live in Rugby in England. Having always lived with lots of people, how would I cope just living with John on our own? Another change in my life to get used to, then having to say the goodbyes to all my friends that I had worked with. My wedding dress cost about £5 which was a lot of money in those days and the bridesmaids dresses were made by a friend of mine.

The great day arrived. I was so nervous waiting for the cars to pick us up. The driver was on time and off to the church we went. This was to be a great day in my life. I can still recall the look on John's face as I walked up the aisle towards him. As I got to his side he smiled and told me how beautiful I was. He looked as handsome as ever. We had a wonderful service and a wonderful reception with the friends I had worked with and my friends from church. In all it was a fabulous day. The time came for us to say goodbye which was hard, and head off to the airport for our honeymoon in London for the first week. My friends arranged for a police escort onto the plane as a joke to make sure I left the Island. To the amazement of John, when we got off the plane at Heathrow airport thinking nothing else could happen as a joke I was wrong. As we were going through customs to see if we had anything to declare, I was called over and asked if I would let them check my suitcase. I made sure they knew we were on honeymoon and was not happy about it, but the law is the law and to the amazement of myself, as I opened my case, out came flimsy underwear attached to slightly blown up balloons, which took off and floated around the building. I can assure you I did not hang around to claim them back as I looked at the shocked expression on John's face. I am sure, because I was the first girlfriend he had, seeing my flimsy underwear floating around the airport would have been a shock to say the least. With much amusement to the staff I closed my case as quick as possible and left the premises with a very red face. This was another joke from my so called friends.

The week in London was great, visiting all the different places, standing at the gates of Buckingham Palace, staring up at Big Ben, on to 10 Downing Street where the Prime Minister lived, then on to Madame Tussauds. We really enjoyed all the sightseeing. There were such interesting places to visit. We did as much as we could fit in that week. It was great getting to know John even more. John did not like the underground tube trains. He said they went too fast for him and did not like getting on and off them, because everyone is pushing to get on or off the train, but over the week he got used to them. Now for the second week, which was spent with Cyril Hocking from Wales, who was the visiting speaker the night I gave my life to Jesus. How strange was that? The family lived on a farm and was I relieved to know I did not have to milk the cows, clean out and feed the pigs, feed the chickens and tether the goats.

John and I had a great time in Wales and through our married life spent many happy holidays in different parts of Wales. We came to love the place and the people there and have made lots of special friends. We got to become great friends with the Hocking family and visited them quite often. During the honeymoon I noticed John was different spiritually than I was. He was in the choir in the church he went to with his uncle Jim, so naturally I thought he must be a Christian, but being in a choir at church does not make you a Christian. You need to repent of your sins and wrongdoings to others and ask Jesus to forgive you and accept Him into your life.

We travelled by train from Wales to Rugby and took a taxi to my mother in law's, where we were going to live, at 7 Steele Street. The number 7 has been my number, it seems, in my life. Born in July, the seventh month, all the time when I was in care homes I was always number 7. I had no proper name as far as the staff were concerned. The youngest of seven girls, the first house of our own was number 7 and in the miracle that took place later on in my life seven things were healed in my body in a few seconds. We lived with my mother in law for about a year and a half. John and I discussed having our own house so we purchased our own house in 7 Newland Street. We were so proud of our first little home. We made do with what little we had as far as furniture was concerned. No credit cards then to use like buy now and pay later. In 1959 we made preparations to start a family. John was still very laid back and had now to get used to living with me on his own, which I can assure you was a battle for him. He was a man of very few words and, I suppose, I made up for that. We had great times together. Everything was fresh and new to us. On December the 19th 1958 I gave birth to my first baby at home in the front room. This seemed to be the norm in those days. Obviously we did not have a scan like you have today. You had to wait until the baby appeared before you knew if you had a boy or a girl. When the midwife announced "you have a baby boy" we were so happy and decided to call him David John. In 1962, I gave birth to my first baby daughter at home. We called her Judith Margaret. The same midwife delivered them both.

As the children were growing up I spearheaded the summer play schemes in the park during the six weeks summer holidays. I would have as many as 200 children from 9am until 4pm Monday to Friday. With the help of the parents and the teenage girls and boys we worked as a team playing team games, also raising money to take them to the seaside for the day, which the children looked forward to each year. I even did this from my wheelchair for a couple of years. The children were very caring towards me. I did this for many years.

Times were hard as we struggled to raise the children and keep the house going and through all of this still getting to know John and his family. John had two sisters, Helen and Barbara, and two brothers, Stewart and Bruce, who passed away with cancer. We had very little furniture; in fact we used a tea chest as a table. My sister in law Ena called me and asked if I could use some second-hand furniture as she was having new furniture. I thought beggars can't be choosers and when you are desperate you are glad of any help, and we agreed the day for the men in the family to deliver it. It was a beautiful day. The lads came with the furniture and they told John and me to take the wardrobe upstairs and they would be sorting the other things out. Our stairs were very steep and had a sharp bend about four steps up.

I said to John, "let's get going then and get the job done". John was dithering about how we were going to manage it, John at one end and me on the other end. We picked the wardrobe up and started up the stairs. As we got to the bend on the stairs John slipped and was lying on the stairs with the wardrobe on top of him. He shouts, "Jean, lift the wardrobe off of me". What a stupid thing to ask a woman, I thought, so I said, "John, I am a woman and cannot lift the wardrobe on my own. Anyway if Popeye was here he could do it because he eats his spinach which gives him strength". John was not amused, to say the least, as you can imagine, but then I saw how funny the situation looked and had a fit of laughter. The men told me to go outside and watch no one stole the things that were still to go into the house. Standing on edge of a roll of carpet minding my own business and passing the time of day, the lads asked me to get off the carpet as they wanted it to put down in the lounge, but hey, where are your manners boys? Say please and you can have the carpet. This banter went on for a few minutes until they gave me the choice of moving off the carpet or they would pull it from under my feet.

As I had a very strong rebellious spirit because of having to stand on my own two feet as a youngster, I stood my ground and did not get off, so they pulled the carpet from underneath me and I fell back, hit my spine on the edge of the pavement, and lay there in agony. They thought I was lying down so as not to do any more work, then they realised I was not playing around and that I was hurt. They picked me up and carried me to my bed. I was in so much pain I could not go to sleep. The next morning John saw to the children for me. He then called for the doctor to come and check me to see if there was any real damage done to my spine. It was Doctor Rogers who came to see me and he told me my back was very badly bruised and things would ease off after a few days' rest. I accepted what he said and rested in bed for three days but things got worse.

6 *Years of Pain and Suffering*

It was just prior to this accident that I started looking for a church to attend and was invited to try a Penticostal Church on Lawford Road in Rugby with a lady called Mrs Tew. I agreed to go along to see what it was like. As I walked into the church as a complete stranger, this woman shook my hand and welcomed me, then gave me a kiss on cheek. Then a man came and shook my hand and gave me a hug. I was not used to this kind of behaviour in a church. I was used to being given a handshake, God bless, and sit down. I told the man in no uncertain manner that I was happily married and did not want strange men giving me a hug. I also thought the women must be lesbians for kissing each other in church. The service began with praise and worship, clapping and dancing. I said to Mrs Tew that it was most irreverent to behave in that way in the house of God, then Pastor Cunningham asked someone to bless the meeting and to my amazement a woman got up and prayed, so I informed her that a woman should be silent with men in the church, but to my astonishment she did not pray in English. Perhaps thinking she could not speak any English, I was informed she was speaking in tongues and was filled with the Holy Spirit. The only spirit I thought of was the spirit drink, and then I am informed someone would interpret the message, which the pastor did. I told John they were stark raving mad at the church and I would find somewhere else to go. Three weeks later I attended that church again and got filled with the Holy Spirit and decided that was the church where God wanted me to be.

Three days after my fall I told John to call the doctor again as my legs were going numb. Doctor Hendry came this time and ordered an ambulance to take me to Saint Cross hospital where I had an x-ray on my back, giving me the result that I had broken the coccyx. I was put on traction for eight weeks to see if it would mend but to no avail, which meant having the coccyx removed. Due to the severity of the impact of the fall it meant having to have three more operations on my spine. I was told I would never walk properly again. I am a fighter and did not accept that from the doctors and I ended up walking with a gait. In and out of hospital, how was John to manage with two children on his own? In the church there was a lovely lady. She introduced herself to us and said she was a foster mother and would help with the children. Her name was Rona Farthing. God definitely sent her to our family. Each time I had to go into hospital Rona would be there to look after the children. In fact she is known as Aunty Rona to my children.

I fell pregnant with my third child and was told I was going to have twins. It was so difficult because I put on so much weight, which put pressure on my spine. I had to go into Saint Mary's hospital for the birth. The first baby died inside me which meant the second baby was pushing away and getting very distressed. The surgeon was called and it was decided that they would have to perform a Caesarean Section to bring the dead baby out and give the other a chance. I did not know that I had got a boy until four days later as I was unconscious for most of those four days. We called him Stephen Thomas. This was 1967. The other twin was a girl. In 1971 I fell pregnant again and was told I was having twins again. This time they booked me for a Caesarean Section to save any complications. I was informed that only one twin survived, and I had a girl. We named her Sharon. The other twin had developed in the fallopian tube and did not survive. That was a boy. Sharon was in the hospital for five months as she had problems feeding. This was a very stressful time for us. Later on I needed a hysterectomy to remove my womb, also another operation to remove my ovaries. This again is where Rona came to look after our children with John. Rona was an angel sent from God. I do not know what we would have done without her help. We still remain good friends to this day.

More surgery and more hospitalisation as I needed surgery to sort out my hammer toes on both feet. This was due to badly fitting shoes as a child. At times I thought no more operations. I have had enough pain and suffering to last a lifetime but there was still more to follow. I know that it was God who held my hand through all of this. Back to the hospital, this time Walsgrave Hospital in Coventry, where the surgeon Mr Whatmore operated yet again, this time putting me in a body cast from my neck, down the trunk of my body and down one leg. This was changed every month. I endured this cast for six months. It was most uncomfortable, to say the least, and very heavy. I was not able to sit so I had to stand with support from crutches or even lie on the floor for comfort. My bed consisted of lying on a large piece of wood placed on the mattress. That was comfort for me. This went on for several years. If I went on holiday we took the board with us. One family we stayed with even took one of her doors off and I slept on that on the floor as it was more comfortable than lying on a soft mattress.

During all this time I attended church, which included leading the Sunday School and the youth on a Wednesday evening. This kept me from wallowing in my own pain and suffering, I enjoyed the work so much. I very seldom missed church. I just had to be in the house of God to praise and worship with the others in the church, many times lying on the floor and praising God. Pastor Cunningham and his wife Lily were like the parents I never had. Their love and kindness to me was far beyond their normal church duties, yet they did it in love. When I was in bed for weeks on end at home, the people would come and have a service in my lounge. I was always uplifted by this and it kept me going from day to day. Lily would come in three times a day to bathe my sore feet and put cream on them. She had a servant heart. There was no doubt about that. It should have been the nurse's job but somehow she always missed my feet. Many people today would not go to church and stand for an hour holding on to crutches leaning against the wall rather than leave the meeting. I needed to be there. It gave me the will to carry on.

Getting into a car was very painful and there were times when I was in the plastercast the men would lay me on the floor of the minibus as I was unable to sit on the seat. The men would take me out of the minibus and carry me into church ready for the service. The Bible teaches in the first chapter in the book of James to consider it pure joy whenever you face trials, because you know that the testing times of your faith makes you stronger.

Some scriptures I found hard to understand at times. How can you consider pain and suffering joy? I did not think it as joy to be suffering all the time and being away from my husband and my children, then as you grow in the faith you understand the Bible better. John never stopped me going to church. I had heard preachers talk about healings and miracles but thought that was only for certain people. It was not for me, even though I was prayed for by men and women of God. I did not get healed because the problem was me. I could not really believe it would happen. Do you ever wonder why some people get all the sickness and some sail through life with none? Well, I did think of that many times. You come to the stage when you think, I cannot take any more, and then another accident happens. Our eldest daughter Judith was a nurse and did her training at Northampton General Hospital. When she had finished her training she decided to come back to Rugby to live. Arrangements were made to collect her plus her belongings. She came and collected Sharon and Stephen, together with myself, to help her carry her belongings to the car. This was difficult for me to get into the car, grimacing with each movement as I positioned myself on the front seat, whilst the children sat on the back seat. We set off to the hospital, had a great drive, arrived and parked the car ready to stack the things in the car. Judith had so much stuff the two children sat in their seats and she piled everything on top of them. I was of no help at all, as I was not going to enjoy another lot of pain and suffering getting out of the car and having to go through the same agony of getting back in the car again.

All set and ready for home and having a laugh at Stephen and Sharon under all the clothes including toys that had been collected, coming through a village we heard a bang then another bang. The car went completely out of control. Judith was a very good driver yet she could not steer the car at all, which was heading for a telegraph pole. My life flashed before me. I thought are we all going to die together in this car and I remember calling aloud to God to help and save us. We had a double blowout on both of the back tyres. There seemed no turning back for us so far away from home. The car finally came to a halt crashing into the telegraph pole breaking it in half. The top half came through the windscreen of the car, pinning me to my seat. I could not move my legs as they were crushed in the mangled front part of the car. I shouted again to God to at least save my children. God heard my cry and all three were thrown out onto the road as the doors of the car were broken off.

Alone in the wrecked car, not able to help my children, was a big problem. No mobile phone like everyone has these days. Where would our help come from? With us crashing into the telephone pole all the household phones were damaged. God, where are you at this time we need You? We need Your help. He did not disappoint us. As Judith was trying to steer the car straight, there were three cars apparently coming in the opposite direction. They stopped their cars at a distance. They thought we were aiming straight at them. In the three cars were medical people who were on their way to the hospital we had just come from, three doctors, three nurses and a nursing sister. What more could God provide at a time like this? These people recognised Judith who was holding her brother and sister's hand in a complete daze. She was calling for help for me. The ambulance people were called, followed soon after by the fire services because they had to cut me from the car. Anyone seeing the state of the car would think nobody came out of that alive. I was semi-conscious all of this time with blood pouring down my face from a big gash on my head and face because my head had gone through the windscreen. I do not remember anything else, only seeing a doctor looking over me and trying to talk to me, asking how I was feeling and what happened. Then I went unconscious again for a while. John was called for, as he was told that I had more damage to my spine, and the x-ray showed that I had a fractured skull. Also I would need surgery to remove splintered glass from the inside of my head. The family waited as the operation took place. They were told that there was a possibility that I would be brain damaged and not remember things. This was not the case. I thank God that He brought me through that and today I can say as I write this book at the age of 76 I am totally sane and of a sound mind. The worse news was to come, that I would need to be in a wheelchair and I would never be able to walk properly again. As the years went by things grew worse. Neither John nor my children could manage me, so it came to the situation of carers coming in and the district nurse had to come most days to give me a wash or a bath, which was a battle at times. The thought of someone else having to do all this was hard to accept, let alone the ordeal of my own children having to do certain duties for me when John was not available, but then when you cannot do things for yourself you do not mind who you call on.

The time I hated being in a wheelchair was when the family took me shopping, people staring at you and not even talking to you. They asked the person pushing the wheelchair if I was alright, how was my pain?, as if I could not answer for myself. The person who is pushing the wheelchair does not have the answers you do. Going into a café I got the same reaction. Does she want tea or coffee? Does she take sugar?, looking at me as if I was some strange person. Your name goes, you feel like a freak, and you just want to go home. I am urging you to speak to the person in the chair first. If they cannot respond then ask the person who is pushing them. It is a lonely life when you are in that situation without people making it worse. The point is you get to the stage when you decide it is better to stay at home than be humiliated in the town.

7 *Desperate for an Answer*

After all the surgery and illness I have had, such as 3 heart attacks, angina, bronchitis, asthma, 3 operations on my spine, operations to my toes, 4 operations on each elbow, removal of my ovaries, 3 operations on my wrists, cataracts on both eyes, appendicectomy, ulcers on my legs, brain surgery to remove glass, tonsils and adenoids,2 operations on my wrist and 2 hysterectomies, do I need to go on? That is not a life to live. I had enough tablets to take to finish my life, and really did contemplate doing it, as I would be out of everyone's way and my family could get on with their lives. Surely there was more to life than living like this, but as a Christian I also knew that God gives life and only takes us to be with Him in His time not ours. I went to meetings where they prayed for the sick to be healed by men who had the gift of healing, men of God like Pastor George Canty, David Willows and Melvin Banks, and many others, but I never got my healing, although there was a calmness that came over me. After my car accident we had a special speaker at our church and I was taken to the service with the view to being prayed for. I sat in my chair like a zombie, not even remembering my full name, and kept falling asleep. Pastor Cunningham asked, did I want prayer? I did not react that well, so he took me to the front and the man prayed for me. I could not really respond because of the state of my mind. An appointment was made for me to go to see a top orthopaedic surgeon by the name of Mr Eisenstein at Oswestry, who after x-rays and other tests gave me the chance of having a fourth operation on my back but did not guarantee a good result, and said that I would have to be away from my family for one year. The other problem, if the operation was not successful, was I could be paralysed over the whole of my body. When you are desperate you reach out for a cure so my name was put on the list to have this done. He really did not want to do it and was offering me nothing that was a concrete answer to my need, yet I was satisfied I had seen the best surgeon there was, who travelled the world operating on people.

Desperation sets in and you think this is never going to happen, for me to be healed, but God has the right time for everything in our lives. We had a little boy called Neil in the Sunday school and he was a horror at times, blocking the toilet pipes with stones and hand towels, causing disruption in the church and even kicking the pastor`s car, making big dents. I suppose he was a replica of what I was like as a child. He would want to pray and I would give him sweets to put him off until the following week in case he used swearwords or said anything else he shouldn't. One Sunday he came into church shouting that he was going to pray. I told him I was boss and it was my choice. He said he would just stand up and say something, and then Pastor Cunningham told him if Aunty Jean said no that was it. He then answered back, "I am going to do it, so shut your mouth." At that moment the Holy Spirit spoke to me and said I was not the one to stop him praying. Prayer was free, but he swears and may embarrass us. I was prompted again by the Holy Spirit that prayer was free, so I called Neil out to the front to pray. This little lad, only three years of age, stands in front of me with hands on his hips and orders the children to shut their eyes. He was going to pray to Jesus. He also told both me and the pastor to shut our eyes.

Little Neil began to pray. "Thank you, Jesus, for bringing us to Sunday School in pastor's old banger; (meaning his car), thank you, Jesus, for the kids here. Some I like, some I hate. You don't mind, Jesus, do you? Only they call me names and pull my hair, that's why I really hate some of them." Neil stopped praying and I asked if he had finished. He told me no, so I told him to shut his eyes again as we were talking to Jesus. He promptly told me to shut mine too. I must admit I felt a bit nervous not knowing what else he was going to pray for. He took my hands as I sat in my wheelchair and was praying for Jesus to heal Auntie Jean. "She be sick a long time, and she do be in a lot of pain, so hurry up, Jesus, do your work and heal her, Amen", and ran back to his seat. God knew this was the right time for me. I had been pointing the finger at Neil and putting him off from praying, but we need to be careful. As we point the finger at someone, there are three fingers pointing back at you. They may have more on you than the finger that is pointing to others. Do not turn a child away if they want to pray for you, as they pray from their hearts. We as adults have to work it all out before we pray as if we have all the answers.

The Lord chose a little rebel to break a big rebel. Believe me I just burst into tears and wept aloud. I asked Pastor Cunningham to take me home. That Sunday night I missed church. I wept as I got before God and repented of the hatred and bitterness I had towards my parents all those years and asked God to cleanse me afresh of all my wrongdoings, then went to bed and had an early night. That night I had two distinctive dreams.

I was not prone to having dreams. In the first dream I was at the hospital having the operation on my spine and I died. The family were standing by my bed crying as the surgeon had told them he could not save me and that my heart could not take the strain. I woke up and was scared to go back to sleep again. I eventually went back to sleep only to have a further dream, but this one was so different to the first one. I was in this big dark place sitting in my wheelchair with twelve other people who were also in wheelchairs and this big tall man, who was foreign by the way he spoke English, prayed for the first lady who got out of her chair then sat down again. The man prayed for her again and she got out of her chair for the second time and walked away, then he came to me put his hands on me and I got out of my wheelchair and was running.I woke up with a start, as you can imagine. Two dreams in one night. In one I die, in the other I live. I could not go off to sleep again and I dare not wake John to tell him about the dreams in case he thought I was going mental.

I kept this to myself until I went to a prayer meeting on the following Tuesday. The pastor saw that I was puzzled and I shared the dreams with them in the church, not knowing if they would believe me or not. The pastor's reply was, this, I am sure, is a sign from God that He is going to heal you. I explained everything that was in the dreams, they were so real. I shared with them that the place I was prayed for was a large dark room with lots of red chairs; the floor was painted black and on the platform was a beautiful blue curtain with writing on it. I also described the man that was in the dream and the accent that he had. I was not sure what to believe about the dreams. One shows me death, the other shows me life. I thought what a contrast between the two.

I was not aware at the time that a youth conference was being arranged by the Assemblies Of God Organisation. It was tickets only so a number of the youth in our church had tickets, so did a number of the adults, to go to this meeting which was to be held in a big hall at the National Exhibition Centre in Birmingham, and there was to be an afternoon and evening meeting. The date for this meeting was March 12th 1988. This was to be a great time for the young people. The travel arrangements were made. My husband John was able to hire a minibus that had a space down the middle for wheelchairs. Some people went in their own cars; the others went in the minibus. John pushed my chair into the minibus and clamped my chair to the floor. I must say that everyone was encouraging me that this could be the day for my miracle, but I was dreading the long journey to Birmingham as every bump in the road that John hit I felt the pain in parts of my body. It seemed a never ending journey.

John was not originally going to stay for the meeting, as he would come back for us, but there was thick fog that suddenly appeared and John had to stay. Because he needed to stay with me he got in free. There was such a feeling of reality as the place I had described to them was staring us in the face, the dark room with the black painted floor and lots of red chairs. People took their seats that were high up and John sat with me at the side downstairs. The meeting started with praise and worship. The place was full to capacity with 12,000 people, then the visiting preacher came onto the platform and took his seat on the platform and started praying. He was asking the Holy Spirit "where is the miracle tonight?" The reply was "the lady in the wheelchair to your left in the green jumper is the miracle tonight", and as he was still praying he saw me get out of my wheelchair and walk.

The preacher was introduced to us as Evangelist Reinhard Bonnke from Germany. The moment that he stood up and began to speak I recognised him to be the man in my dream. I could not believe this was happening. He began to preach with power. You could feel the anointing in the place. I was glad that John heard the gospel as he had not given his life to Jesus yet. An altar call was made for people to surrender and give their lives to Jesus. Young people and adult people swarmed to the front, throwing syringes used for drugs and packets of cigarettes onto the platform. As they came to repent they were asked to repeat a prayer, and then were sent off to a room to be given a booklet and have a little talk. There was a break before the evening meeting. One of the stewards named Pat took me to the toilet. She was on her knees weeping as she saw how I struggled. She was calling God, "if you can heal this woman, please do." Then she took me back to where John was waiting for me. He was looking very worried and asked was I alright. I assured him I was alright. People were milling around talking to each other while I was thinking, what if nothing happens tonight and I go home in the same condition as I came? But then I thought this was a big ordeal, even for the Lord, as I had so much wrong with me and I had never read in the Bible where Jesus healed so many things all at once. Well, okay Lord, even if you heal one thing that is wrong with me, perhaps the others will follow. I suppose I was like doubting Thomas in the Bible, because we all have these doubts what God can do. The evening started again with praise and worship, then Reinhard preached the gospel again and made another altar call when yet again more people gave their lives to Jesus. They prayed the prayer of repentance, had the little book given them, and went to speak with a counsellor, then came back into the arena. Reinhard was then informed that he only had ten minutes left as the place had to be vacated. He thought, wow, I have not prayed for the sick and I do not have the time left to speak about healing. I must just pray. I was still thinking, is this my time for something to happen? Well, God did not disappoint me. God certainly has a sense of humour because we hated the Germans during the occupation in Jersey, yet He chose a Pastor from Germany, Reinhard Bonnke, to pray for me. Once I would have hated him, now it is God`s love that I have for him.

8 *My Miracle Takes Place*

Reinhard prayed for a lady who was sitting in middle aisle in her wheelchair. He said, "In the name of Jesus stand up". With this she stood up, then promptly sat back down in her chair, then Reinhard came from off the platform and went to that lady and prayed again. She got up from her chair and as he was still praying she walked slowly to the front with her hands in the air thanking God for her healing. I could just see a little of what was going on and the thought came, that is exactly what happened in my dream. Reinhard remembered what the Holy Spirit had shown him when he was praying. He thought, that is not the woman that I was shown, so he ran over to where I was and said, "I believe you are going to be healed". My reply was, "I know, I know, I know". He did not ask my name or ask what was wrong with me. He told me to stand up in the name of Jesus. John could not believe he was saying this, as he told Reinhard that I could not stand, and not to be stupid. I was paralysed from my waist down and, after all, he was protective of me. I told him it was alright and to calm down. John had never been to a meeting like it before, so he did not know what to expect.

Reinhard continued to pray for me, and as I came out of the chair I fell to the ground to his amazement. Thinking, oh no, what have I done? I looked up at him and he asked me how I was. I replied it felt as if I was under an anaesthetic. His reply was, "Doctor Jesus is operating on you". He helped me to stand and continued to pray for the power of God to go into my legs. I felt as if my body was being pulled in all directions. My back that was bent over was straightened up. The left leg which was two inches shorter than the other leg was normal. I had difficulty breathing. I could breathe with no discomfort, my eyesight was restored to full sight, full strength in both my legs, as Reinhard prayed again and told me to walk in the name of Jesus. John looked horrified and told him I had not been able to walk for many years and what if she falls? Reinhard comforted John to tell him he would be ready to catch me if I fall. The power of God hit me like a bolt of electricity and I was off like a rocket and ran the whole way round the arena, praising God and crying with joy. There was Holy Ghost pandemonium in the place, people standing on their chairs to get a better view of what was going on. I just wanted to get back to John to see how he was. Reinhard was shouting, "where is that woman?" I was pushing my way through the crowds to get to him and he started asking me what had happened to me, and as I was talking to him, John came towards me and we kissed and hugged each other with tears of joy streaming down our faces. John's words to me were, "I never want to see you so ill again".

John and I were invited onto the platform to let the people see what God had done. They had seen a miracle right before their eyes. Reinhard asked me what had been wrong with me, and then he asked me to give the people a demonstration, so I ran again in a circle around the platform and the people just went wild. What I wanted to do was to go to the people from my church and give them all a big hug, for they are the ones who had been there for me for

25 years of pain and suffering. One young lad touched my heart as he shared how he was going to go back into the world as he was bored with church and he saw nothing to change his mind. He saw a miracle that amazed him and we had our photograph taken together. The journey home was different as we rejoiced and clapped our hands. I kept standing up. I did not want to sit down. John had to go back to Birmingham for the wheelchair as I had to return it to the hospital in Rugby. This was all captured on camera by someone and later made into a video called 'Something to Shout About', followed a little later on with a second one 'Standing The Test Of Time', then as time went by they were put together on a DVD which is still selling as I am writing this book. It is a wonderful tool for evangelism and many people have been saved and healed through watching it. The sale money goes back into the ministry to Christ for all Nations at Halesowen which is the ministry of Evangelist Reinhard Bonnke, together now with his co-worker Daniel Kolenda.You can purchase it by phoning 0121 602 2000.

On arrival at the house I jumped out of the minibus, let myself into the house and went straight up the stairs to the bathroom. My youngest daughter Sharon was still living at home and was there with her boyfriend. She thought a burglar had entered the house but the lad was too afraid to check. He said to Sharon that it could be her mother, and Sharon`s reply was, "my mother is crippled and cripples don't run up stairs". I ran down the stairs shouting, "When Jesus heals cripples they can do anything". When Sharon saw me she just hugged me and wept. I shared with her what had happened. She was so happy for me, in fact all the family were, as they would be free from having to look after me. I still had to sleep on the board that night as we needed a new mattress. I slept like a baby as the saying goes, then waking next morning I checked with John this was not another dream and he confirmed with me it was real. He was there to witness it all.

Sunday morning and through the day I was going to enjoy my freedom, doing the jobs I had not done for a long time, getting busy with the breakfast, then preparing the lunch, feeling so free. My son Stephen called to see if I needed anything doing and could not believe what he saw as I was working away in the kitchen. Time to go to church. Pastor Cunningham phoned and said he would pick me up in his car. I promptly told him that I wanted to use my legs and walk to the church, which was quite a way down the road from our house. As I started walking down the hill to the church there was a strange rattling sound coming from behind me. When I looked back there was John with the wheelchair in case I fell. He was told to take it back to the house, things were alright. There was elation at the service, in fact a riot, as we danced and sang praises to God in thanks for what had happened the previous night.

Time for the Sunday School children to come and I can still see the expression on my grandchildren's faces as they saw me walking normally, running about. They ran out to my daughter Judith and were shouting, "Mummy, you should see Nanny, she is running around and she is walking". My daughter Judith's reply was "Nanny cannot walk or stand, so do not be silly". They wanted her to see for herself. When she saw me she wept with joy and we just hugged each other. She still could not believe it until I turned up on her doorstep next day for tea. Little Neil came into the church and looked at me and just said, "What happened? You are better". I told him Jesus heard the prayer he prayed for me in church six weeks earlier and healed me. He was so pleased. He wanted to know if he was naughty in class, would I be nice to him? When I told him if he was naughty he would still be put on the chair at the back, Neil's reply was, "just try it, and if you get sick again, I won't pray for you". He had an answer for everything. Neil used to remind me for a while, when it was his birthday, that he did pray for me and Jesus did heal me. His treat was a trip to Macdonald's.

Monday was the day John would collect the children's allowance, together with a weekly pension for me to help with the extra care I had. On the Monday I went to the Post Office to fetch it myself. As I stood in the queue waiting my turn people were asking if I had a twin sister. My reply was, no, this is me, I had a miracle healing on Saturday and do not need my wheelchair. Their reply was, "well, you won't need your sick money any more". I could not draw that money because with my mouth confessing I am healed, and yet drawing a sickness pension, it was not a good witness, so I sent the book back to the pension people. It took them seven months to accept I was completely well and for Doctor West to confirm it. What would I do now? To pass the time away I decided to go on a voluntary basis each day and help on the ward at the hospital where I had spent so many years, wanting to help others that were sick, just sitting with them until they went for their operations and being there for them when they got back, also doing odd jobs to help the nurses. The hospital Chaplain would ask me to go and pray for people with him. This was certainly a new life for me. The day I gave my life to Jesus He gave me a heart of love and compassion for others and took away the heart of anger, hatred and bitterness. My life was changed, to the Glory of God.

A week after my healing I went to see Doctor West as I had an appointment with him. As I walked into the area where I had to book in, the secretary looked at me in astonishment and asked, had I got a twin sister?, as the week before she had seen me in my wheelchair. Now she is looking at a woman who looks like her but is now standing in front of her. The puzzled look on her face was something to see. I told her I was the same lady from last week's appointment. When my name was called I told her not to say anything to the doctor, as I wanted to see the surprise on his face. As I walked in he was still writing the last patient's notes up. He told me not to come to the surgery again, as it was too much for me, and that in future he would visit me at home, to which I replied "you need not bother, just look up and see". He looked at me and went, "Wow, how did this come about? Had I been to another doctor?" My reply was "yes, Doctor Jesus, who gave me a miracle".

He then told the secretary to watch that I did not leave the surgery as he wanted this to be checked with his colleague Doctor Sharman. They were discussing me, and Doctor Sharman said he had seen me and I was looking so much younger and very fit, to which Doctor West replied it must be a miracle then. The two doctors had me running up and down stairs, running outside on the pavement, even bending up and down, touching my toes. Doctor West retired from the surgery group and sadly Doctor Sharman went to be with Lord after an illness. I attended his funeral and was delighted to hear from his best friend that he became a Christian through watching the video of my miracle. His father was a Baptist Minister and showed the same video in his church, as he prayed for the sick and believed in healing and miracles. Over the months Doctor West confirmed that he could not fill in the form for me to renew my mobility claim, as I was no longer disabled. That is all I needed. I did not need any other doctor to discredit what God had done for me. My doctor knew what I had gone through and certainly no surgeon operates on a person for the sake of it or to keep the patient happy. I certainly was not faking any of my illnesses. Why would I want to put my family through all that, for they saw what I went through and heard the cries of pain as I tried to move around? I feel sorry for such people. How can you preach from the Bible yet pull God's miracles apart? By His stripes I was healed completely. I was also checked at Oswestry Orthopaedic hospital by Mr Eisenstein and two other doctors and discharged as completely fit after having a little jog with them in the hospital grounds.

A couple of months after my healing there was a Fire Conference at the National Exhibition Centre in Birmingham. The visiting speaker was Evangelist Reinhard Bonnke. People travelled from all over the world to come to it. I was sitting by a very distinctive gentleman with big bushy eyebrows on the front row. I was given a pass as a guest. In the afternoon session Reinhard called me onto the platform to interview me and to demonstrate I was still able to run. The reaction from the people was tremendous. It seemed to lift the people's spirits to a degree of expectation to receive something special. The very distinguished looking man with big bushy eyebrows I had been sitting next to was Pastor Oliver Raper Senior. He has a beautiful wife called Ria. After Reinhard had interviewed me he prophesied over me saying, "Jean Neil, I believe in my heart that the Lord has a ministry for you, a Holy Ghost ministry, not to comfort the sick, says the Lord, but to heal the sick and many signs will follow you". He laid hands on my head and I fell onto the floor under the anointing of God. I was helped up off the floor by Oliver Raper Junior who was in charge of the running the Christ For All Nations office in Halesowen at the time, and Peter Van Den Berg who travels with Reinhard on his crusades. They both escorted me back to my seat. God spoke to Pastor Raper Senior to invite me over to South Africa to tell my story.

About a month later I was invited to speak in a little hall in Birmingham by Pastor George Canty. I was nervous as I had never spoken in front of a crowd at another church before. The Lord was with me that night as I gave my story to people then I went to sit down. George asked what I was doing, so I replied, I am sitting down as I had finished what he had asked me to do. His reply was, "Jean, you don`t think God has raised you out of your chair for nothing. You are going to pray for the sick". I could not believe what he was saying. I had never prayed for the sick in public before, let alone lay hands on people. I said that I would watch him. It would be like a practice. "It is not a practice, you have been given the gift to pray for the sick and you have the anointing to do so". God was going to show me big things.

He called people forward for prayer and told me to pray for the person in front of me. The person in front of me was a gentleman. I followed him from his feet upwards. He was big and very tall. I looked at George with a smile on my face, reminding him that he had said God was going to show me big things. The man told me he was nearly seven foot tall and had frozen shoulders. Of course this puzzled me, how to reach him, so thinking to stand on a chair would be the answer George put me right on that point, and with quick thinking told the man to kneel, then I could reach his shoulders. George corrected me again and told me the man did not have to kneel, just to take his hands and pray. Being a bit annoyed with George, as this was my patient and he had his, and I would pray as I felt led, taking the man's hands prayed something and this big man fell to the floor on his back. Looking at George and remarking, if God has healed this man's shoulders he now probably has a damaged spine, I was told to leave him on the floor. Within ten minutes he was standing up with both hands in the air praising God. He was to have had surgery on the following Monday and was able to go to the hospital to be checked and discharged. The other miracle was his wife, who was in a wheelchair. She was healed and she gave her life to the Lord. Only the Lord touched her, no one else.

It was there that I met Stan and Jean Taylor. We became very good friends. Stan was Pastor George Canty`s chauffeur over the years, driving him to various meetings whilst Jean would look after Mrs Canty, especially in her last years. I have travelled around different parts of the United Kingdom giving my story and praying for the sick, also leading many people to the Lord at different venues and churches, speaking at Women Aglow, Men`s breakfasts, youth meetings and even at school assembly. To tell of all I have seen God do would need a book on its own, but I will mention a few of them.

In Nottingham a little boy named Joshua came to a meeting with his mother. His toes were septic and bleeding and he had no toenails. The specialist who was on Joshua`s case suggested the he may have to operate on his feet. A week later, after prayer, his feet were completely healed and his nails grew as normal. In fact, his mother had to cut his toenails three times in one week.

In Dorset a lady on drugs and suicidal was released, set free and healed. Also another lady was set free from witchcraft and the clutches of the devil. A Pastor's son who was born with a deformed finger was healed overnight. Over the years blind eyes have been opened, the deaf have heard, the lame have walked and people have been raised from their wheelchairs. There have been many more things that have happened, even barren women giving birth after being told they could not have children. People with drinking and smoking problems have been set free. People with marriage problems have had their marriage mended. I know people question why do some get healed and others do not, but I have thought about this, and I feel that if everyone that we prayed for was healed we would become complacent and forget the love and compassion that goes with praying for the sick. For some it is a choice between being healed and losing the mobility benefit that there is. I was glad to have my freedom and give up my mobility. We are not God, just vessels doing the work He has called us to do.

A lady from Birmingham came into the church in her wheelchair, which she had used for some time. When the time came to pray for the sick she was first in the line because she really felt something was going to happen. As she was watching the video, I prayed for her, then went on to pray for others, then there was a big cheer as she got up from her chair, walked around the room with nobody holding her, then she did a little run. When the time came for her to go home she was offered a lift from a friend but she left the chair at the church and chose to walk home. I was so surprised the next day to get a phone call saying she wanted to go back in her wheelchair as she had been thinking of all the things she would have to give up and the things she would miss. The last one was she would miss the people taking pity on her and they would stop speaking to her and visiting her. I know what I preferred. I hated the staring and the pity. That is what she chose and went back into the wheelchair and was worse.

One outstanding healing was a young girl from Russia who was adopted by an English family when they found her lying in the street in a terrible state. Her parents had abandoned her because she was born with disjointed hips and deformed feet and was unable to walk or stand. She was brought to live in England. The family had a daughter of their own and the two girls really bonded with each other. The disabled girl came to the church where I was speaking together with the family. On the Saturday she asked her adopted mum if her sister could take her uptown in her chair. Mum agreed and off they went to buy some pretty socks with frilly tops and a pair of patent leather shoes. She had a vision of being healed that weekend. The hips would be healed on the Saturday and her feet on the Sunday.

When I saw her on the Saturday at the meeting all I knew was that she had a special support on her hips and she had to sit or lie on the floor to relieve the discomfort she was in. Her parents knew nothing of the plans and also hid what they had got from the shops. The time came to pray for the sick. She shuffled to the front. As I prayed for her the power of God touched her in a mighty way. I carried on praying with people. This young girl shuffled to the toilet, took off her support, and shuffled back shouting she was healed. She could not stand as her feet were so deformed they were almost back to front. On Sunday evening she was out at the front again. We watched as her feet were being healed in front of our eyes. Off to the toilet with her sister and she came back into the church a very happy little girl wearing her new socks and a beautiful pair of patent shoes, walking with help from her sister and just praising God. It was just amazing to see the joy on her face. I recall another girl that night being totally healed

of a very bad squint in both her eyes. God is a God
of miracles.

The tent crusades in Wales with Marilyn Harry and
Maldwyn Jones were an experience. On one occasion,
working with Maldwyn, I was left to pray for the sick and
fifteen young lads came to me and said one of them was
very sick. I noticed they had put powder on his face to
look pale. I realised what they were up to, so I thought
would shock them a bit as I explained the lad needed to
get to the doctor very soon as he did not look as if he had
long to live. They looked very shocked at my reaction. I
said, "you are being very stupid, you are not mocking me
but God and God does not take too kindly to that sort of
behaviour". They really must have been afraid. They were
not laughing now and two boys began to cry and say sorry.
The joy was in the tent as they all gave their lives to Jesus.
Things are not always straightforward in the ministry. You
really have to be led by the guidance of the Holy Spirit for
answers. As the ministers from different churches called
me to give my story and pray for the sick, in every church
we saw people's lives being changed and healings taking
place. It is impossible to mention everyone who I have
met, so please forgive me for not mentioning your name
personally, but I love you all. Two people in Hull I want
to mention, Joy who my family stayed with many times,
and a lady called Maria, who was in a wheelchair and
is still looking to God for her healing. Both these ladies
have been an inspiration to me as they have been through
so much and do not give up on their miracles.

Scotland was another place that I was invited to minister.
There again the power of God moved in a mighty way.
A lady was healed of breast cancer. A couple's marriage
mended. Two young people came back to the Lord after
they started taking drugs and getting drunk most nights.

Seeing God move in different ways is intriguing, to say the least. You never know what will happen in any of the meetings.

I had an invitation to go to London to speak on the Revelation programme, which was hosted by Howard Conder. I travelled by train with my friend Rosemary to get to the place for the evening broadcast. When we arrived it seemed everything was going wrong as the electric power failed and the computers were down. It seemed that we were destined to go back home and make another visit another time. As we prayed the Lord overruled on the power and everything was back on. Howard interviewed me, then we had people phoning in with needs for prayer. A lady called in to say she was healed as I spoke, and gave thanks to God then went off line, and then she called in again to ask if I would pray for a friend of hers, who could not have children. As I started praying she was amazed to hear me mention her friend's name as she had not given it to me, she just said her friend. The cameraman felt the Holy Spirit so strongly he could hardly stand and was swaying all over the place. The people on the sound desk in another room said they were glued as it were to their seats because of the anointing that came over the system. Rose and I got to Rugby very late, or should I say, the following morning. When I got in the house and looked at the answer machine flashing away I said to Rosemary I will check them later, which I did. The machine was full to capacity and could take no more. I have done several radio broadcasts over the years including question time.

9 *Travelling Abroad*

My first visit abroad was to South Africa for a whole month. This was my first time away from John since we got married and I wondered how we both would cope. This was arranged with Christ for All Nations and Jessica Raper. The team travelled with me, led by Pastor Oliver Raper Senior. His son, who was also called Oliver, came as he was in charge of the office in England. He told me there was one thing I had to do and that people would not believe I had been to South Africa and that was to ride an ostrich. Me ride that silly bird, I do not think so. He convinced me this was right. It was a long flight to Johannesburg. From there we travelled by road to the following places: Pretoria, Durban, East London, Grahamstown, Port Elizabeth, Utenhage, Adelaide, Wilderness, Mosselbay, George and through to Cape Town then travelling back up to Table Mountain where I went to the top by cable car. This was a sight to behold, just viewing the beauty from the height of that beautiful mountain on through the Cape Province to the Orange Free State to Bloemfonten, on to Welkom, Kimberley, back to Johannesburg travelling to Gormiston and Soweto. It was a lot of travelling, sleeping as we went from one place to the other. It was amazing how my body battery was charged to do what the Lord wanted me to do each day. A day at the Kruger Park was a day I shall never forget seeing the creation of all the wild animals.

We were not disappointed as we saw what God was doing. As we went from church to church they were packed to capacity, with people with great expectation of what was going to happen and they were not disappointed. At one meeting a young girl who was born deaf cried out she could hear. In another meeting two ladies came to me. They were identical twins. They told me they would love to have children but they could not conceive no matter what they tried. I told them to fetch their husbands and I would pray for them. Before I started to pray the Holy Spirit prompted me to tell God what they wanted and to and to say how many. The one twin said she wanted triplets and all girls, so the other twin agreed that was what she wanted. Pastor Raper stood back and jokingly said he was having nothing to do with it as it meant six more children in Africa. I prayed and their prayers were answered. They both conceived on the same night, both went into labour on the same day in the same hospital, and both gave birth to triplets. All six were girls.

I had an opportunity to minister in Pastor Ray McCauley's church and Pastor Raper suggested I did a demonstration run along the front of the church then up the middle aisle. Pastor Ray had different plans for me. It was to pretend to do what Pastor Raper had told me to do then turn back and run around the whole of the church but even the best of plans do not always go accordingly, because they forgot to unplug the microphone from me and as I started running there was this loud bang. There were sparks behind me. Everyone was laughing. It must have looked really funny at the time. When the time came to pray for the sick Pastor Ray called people to the front to make a line and mentioned Jean will come along the line and pray for you. Not realising the steps to the platform folded in under it, I went to step onto them. I fell off the platform so they prayed for me first. I went down under the power of God and the people had to wait for me. I was so fired up with a mighty anointing that people were going down on the floor and being healed as I went along the row, young people weeping as they gave their lives to Jesus.

It seemed I was never going to get the chance to ride an ostrich as we were either too early at the farm or too late. On the very last part of that stretch of the journey we saw this ostrich farm. They were Christian people that owned the farm. We asked about the chance to ride the bird, only to be told they were not bringing them out that day. The disappointment showed on my face as that was my last chance and by this time of the crusade I was really feeling homesick and missing John and the family. They asked the men if they would let me have a go and the answer was yes, but you will have to learn how to sit on the ostrich, so I practiced on a male bird, then they put me on a female bird, no reins to hold on to, just holding the bird's wings. They tapped her on the back and off she went with me screaming my head off as they released twelve male ostriches which chased her. These birds can do thirty to forty miles an hour in speed because they race them. It took three men to catch hold of her and stop her, then with a big grin on the team's faces as they said it was a joke. I must say they did repent. I have done a parachute jump, done hang gliding, been in an air balloon, ridden in a helicopter, but there is one thing I want to do on the next visit to South Africa, that is to abseil down Table Mountain. I have that urge every time I visit there.

I learnt so much on that trip as I was taught by Pastor Raper, who is a man mightily used of God and certainly knows his Bible inside out and preaches with sound teaching. His wife Ria is a lovely lady and I have stayed at their home on many occasions. On my visits to South Africa they call me 'daughter' and I refer to them as 'mum and dad' and have a great respect for them both. There have been many visits to South Africa, including going to pray for the ex president and his wife and having tea with them. The house was heavily guarded with security men at all times.

The latest visit was this year in March, arriving in Cape Town. I was with my friend Caroline. I will write an extract from Pastor Paul Raper from his report. The trip started in Cape Town on the 4th of March to deep into the frontier country of the Eastern Cape, ending 4th April in Port Elizabeth, travelling over 3000 kilometres. The first service was in the open air, the weather very warm, then in the evening it went so cold my teeth were chattering and a lady gave me her coat to wear. I gave a little talk saying how I had forgiven the ladies who were cruel to me, when suddenly this young lad rushed forward, fell prostrate on his face and wept aloud, crying he needed to repent as he had stabbed a lad the night before and left him for dead and he needed to own up to the police. I came from the platform and prayed with him. Then he gave his life to Jesus and went to the police to give himself up. There were other meetings in a large auditorium hosted by Dr Gustav Du Toit. God touched many lives as they heard about the miracle in Jean's life. The journey took us to many different churches, some large some small. God sees the people, not the size of the building. Through to George to visit Pastor Raper Senior and also ministered in the Mosselbay area.

From George and the Southern Cape we travelled the scenic Garden Route, through Knysna and Plettenburg

Bay to Port Elizabeth. Jean and Caroline walked many miles each day next to the Indian Ocean, enjoying God's creation. People were very responsive to the word and the call of God on their lives and being set free from the things they held on to. A lovely visit to Addo Elephant Park for the day, then the next meeting was in a little tin shack where we saw the powers of darkness as a man manifested like a madman. The pastor asked me to go down and minister to him and after a short while he was set free and I even danced with him. People were saved and healings took place. God is not a God of confusion.

On to the Eastern Cape, to the towns of Bedford and Adelaide, where the Christians had been praying and fasting prior to our arrival. The cry was, "God, send us revival". Amid thunderstorms and heavy rain showers people came and God touched lives mightily. They were not disappointed. Bodies lay on the floor, as God was setting them free. A mother and father asked me to pray for their new born baby who was not expected to live. Caroline and I went to the hospital and prayed for the baby, who was in an incubator. We went the following day to pray again and the doctors could not believe the change in the baby. The baby was allowed home to his parents within the week and he is doing well as I write this passage. Our hosts were David and Mary Khoury, the most humble people I have met. Their love and compassion for people flows from them to see people's lives changed. David is an artist. His paintings and his eye for art and beauty is wonderful. I have one such piece in my lounge. May God continue to bless these two people who believed for God to do something in Bedford.

Dr Kruger and his wife took us to a senior care home to show the DVD. In the anointed evening meeting a young girl had her deaf ears opened. She was deaf from birth.

She wrote on a piece of paper that she saw Jesus by her bed and she could hear what He was saying to her, and said she was going to get healed on the very day that she was healed. The final meeting, I must confess, was for the young people at the Nelson Mandela Metropolitan University. Jon Paul Raper invited the students to the meeting, Christians and non Christians came, the numbers seemed to keep growing until there was no more room. Jon Paul is a young man on fire for God and just wants to do His work. The students were on fire for God and some committed their lives to Jesus. What a joy it was to minister to these students. There were twenty-seven official meetings and home visits. In fact the final count was 44 meetings. Caroline and I were ready for home and a good rest.

There were many visits to the Isle of Wight hosted by Ian and Julie Gutteridge. John loved the Island and we made friends with Joyce and Steve Taylor, John and Kath Urry, and many lovely people as I ministered in the different halls and churches. Many lives were changed and people saved including a lady who heard me speak in a bar. As we showed the video other people who were having a drink could not resist peeping round the screen to see what we were doing and to see people going down on the floor as they were being prayed for. One day it was decided that we would all dress up and be pirates. This was a great day. Ian made me walk the plank, as it were, because I laughed at him when it was supposed to be serious. His wife took pity on me and said she would take my place, so she climbed the scaffolding to be alongside me, then Ian suggested if Julie could make me say sorry we would both be free. Being a rebel I said no, so he said the consequence was he would throw a bucket of water over both of us. I thought it would be a bucket with paper in it as he would not dare throw the water over his wife, but he was true to his word. The bucket was full of water and as he threw the water I ducked and Julie got most of it over her. I retaliated later and threw a bucket of water over him, much to his dismay. I spoke at the prisons on the Island. In fact I have done so in a number of prisons where Myra Hindley was, and I have also met the Kray brothers. I do not go into these places to judge or point the finger but to speak about the love of God to them and many have become Christians and have changed their lives for the good. I say to them there but for the grace of God go I, because the way my life was going I would have been in such a place myself.

The Elim Church I attend go on trips to help the people in Romania and I went on one of these trips. We had all paid our own costs and also raised extra money of our own to be able to use where best needed. Something like this changes your life and makes you thankful for what you have, as these people have very little and yet are prepared to share the little they have with you. The purpose is to clean up old houses and put electricity in them, also dig and sort out sanitation for the toilet. Taking food parcels is a weekly trip and a medical team visit the sick. The gypsy children are very friendly and when you visit them they look for sweets and presents. They have very little yet they are so happy. On that visit I was coming out of the minibus and as the children were pushing to come into the bus I was pushed and fell out onto the grass, got up brushed myself down and accepted the invitation to ride one of their horses bareback. Off I went, enjoyed the ride, got back to the group and my wrist was very swollen. The doctor at camp took me to the hospital next morning and the x-ray showed a fracture. No more hard work for me as my arm was in plaster. If ever you have the chance to go to Romania you will not be disappointed. In fact two families from our church went out there to live and help the people.

10 *Hotel Experience*

An invite to America was a daunting thought; I would be travelling on my own to all these different places, doing two flights per day, not understanding the different meanings to things we say. Anyway Christ For All Nations arranged all the air tickets for me. The majority were for me to fly with the airline called Delta. At times I was beginning to think there was no such airline, although they had the name up at the airports, yet every time I was being told that my flight was not going, and they would put me on another flight. I was travelling from Dallas to my next destination and back to Dallas. This went on for ten days. I visited so many different places and churches, went on the 700 Club in Virgin Beach Virginia, meeting Pat Robertson, also many radio interviews. I did manage the odd flight on Delta, which was often too rare. On one flight they promised they would upgrade the class I was in, but I was satisfied my seat was there for me. As we took off and had been flying for a while my name was called to go to the front of the plane. There was no way I was going to move from my seat. The steward came and told me that I had got a complimentary seat first class. As I got to my seat I noticed this film star sitting in the front row with a young lad. I knew his face but only thought of Moses. Yes, you have guessed, it was none other than

Charlton Heston, who called me to sit by him and his son as his guest. Asking me what I was doing travelling alone I wasted no time giving him my story and signed a book of mine called I Experienced a Miracle. When the plane landed he escorted me through the building to wait for the people who were to meet me.

One of the places I was to speak at was in Chicago. I had a night flight arriving at the airport at 4am in the morning then a two hour journey by taxi to the hotel that I was to stay at for the one day and night. God blessed me with a Christian taxi driver who saw me to the hotel and asked the porter to look after me. He took me to sign in and get my key. Doing this so many times, surely nothing could go wrong? I had got a TV interview at lunchtime. They asked how the bill was being paid. I told them the Pastor from the church where I was going to speak that night would be in to cover the cost. I was left waiting some time. The lady who was dealing with me told me she would be holding my passport and I would be under hotel arrest until things were sorted out. Even phoning the TV people it seemed they still did not accept what I was saying. From 6am to lunchtime I sat with two security men. I had no food, not even a drink of water. It was one of the Hilton Hotels. By this time I called Christ for All Nations and said that I wanted to come home to England. They called the Pastor and made a complaint to the hotel management then moved me to another hotel.

Arriving at the next hotel, noticing it was another Hilton Hotel, I was a bit dubious. Being met by the manager I was told there will be no cost to anyone, it was compliments of the hotel. What a difference of service. This was first class. The Pastor collected me for the meeting. The anointing and power of God was in that meeting. I could hardly stand as I was praying for the sick. A young girl who was almost blind shouted she could see clearly. A woman who had a big goiter on her neck felt something happening. When she took the scarf from her neck the swelling was completely gone. Two ladies came for prayer to have children. Both have beautiful children, even after being told they would never conceive. Back to the hotel for a good night's sleep. I came down for breakfast next morning only to be told, 'no taxis', the drivers are on strike. A limo was waiting to take me, together with the Pastor and his wife, to the airport and bring them back compliments of the Hilton.

What a drive we had, chocolates, champagne and then I was told to call my family and speak to them to cheer me up. I arrived at the airport only to see two porters rushing to take my case. I got to the Delta desk only to be told my flight was cancelled. We prayed hard and I was put on another flight straight away, landed the other end and went to fetch my case. My case was still at Chicago airport. The shops were closed so I could not get anything to change into. I had a meal, then off to the church and was amazed to see Ray Macauley at the same church. What a meeting we had. Three children were healed of their deformed bodies; people cried to God for salvation, people were really fired up. The other miracle was the airline people had flown my case on a special flight as I was moving on to another part of the country.

The next church was in Texas. It was Valentine's day. The church was decorated with flowers and balloons. I had breakfast with all the governing board, the Pastor and his wife. Boxes of chocolates were handed round to greet each one as they sat down. Praise and worship songs were based on the love of Jesus. I was amused the way I was introduced onto the platform. The Pastor said, "We are very happy to have Jean with us all the way from England. We have had breakfast with her and she is quite a gal, in fact she has got spunk". He explained that it was 'get up and go and full of energy' after he saw my red face. There was a homeless person who used to come to that church every Sunday and sit on his own. The Sunday I was there was no different. As I made the appeal for salvation and healing he ran to the front and fell on his knees. Weeping he gave his life to Jesus and asked if he could say something. He shared that he came to church to pass the time away. He saw people praising God, clapping and dancing, being all spiritual, then at the coffee break heard people talking about each other and saw nothing to change him, but he heard a story of a life that was changed from hatred to love and he could feel the love of God was real. It was what he had been waiting for. We need to watch our actions in the meeting and when we are having the coffee break we are being watched by others. That man smartened himself up in every way and was a real help in the church. Too many churches to mention, but we saw the hand of God in all situations. Twenty flights in ten days was to be too much for me. I was so jet lagged and had to cancel the visit to Canada. In the last meeting a lady came forward for prayer. She had three large cancer growths on her leg. They looked terribly painful. As I prayed with her she fell to the floor and lay there for some time. When she stood up she told me she felt funny sensations in her legs. The cancer growths were still on her legs. It seemed nothing had changed until the next day. She came with her husband to the hotel where I was staying and showed me the cancer growths that had fallen off her legs during the night. Just the slight scars were to be seen on her legs where the growths had been. I rejoiced with them and thanked the Lord for the miracle.

One place I was never going back to was Jersey. God had different plans for me. When the video was made into a DVD many people had it given to them for Christmas. Several phone calls came to ask whether I would be prepared to go back Jersey to tell my story. The answer was definitely not, as I never wanted to go back. I would rather preach to the Eskimos. These calls kept coming. The answer was the same. After receiving one of these calls, I began to sing the words of an old gospel hymn, "Then my soul shall fear no ill, Jesus lead me where you will, I will go without a murmur". Straight away the Lord spoke to me, "what about Jersey then?" I was only singing as the words came to me, "well don't sing them if you don't mean it". What a shock that was. The call back to that lady was okay, I will come but still deep down I was feeling very apprehensive of going.

All the arrangements were made as John and I travelled by car to Weymouth for the fast ferry. When we arrived we were told the ferry had been cancelled due to high winds and storms. I was quite pleased as there was still that little bit of me saying go back home, when over the loudspeaker came a voice asking John and myself to go to the booking office. Thinking to myself, maybe there has been a mistake with the bookings, I was told that tickets had been purchased for us on the night ferry. I was quite happy for someone else to go in our place and wait for the ferry the next day. They were sworn to secrecy regarding who paid for the tickets. I did not sleep that night thinking what there was to face. We arrived at Jersey harbour at 8am. It was a beautiful day. As I stepped off the ferry my whole body went into a stiff spasm and I could not move, and then started vomiting badly. The steward fetched the people we were staying with and they prayed with me.

There were posters everywhere stating Jersey Girl Comes Home To Tell Her Story. The first meeting was at La Rocquier School. The place was absolutely packed to

capacity. I wanted to run away. It was a strange feeling
to be giving my story in the very island where all these
things happened. What if any of the people were there
that worked in the home? One person I was pleased to see
was the lady who prayed for me to come to know Jesus as
my saviour. She had one big hug from me. Tears flowed
down my face as the story unfolded. This became a reality
standing up in front of all these people who needed to
know the truth of what it was like in the girls' home and
what we went through. This touched many people's lives.
As they gave their lives to Jesus people were being healed
from hurting hearts. One lady I met seemed to have a
special bond with me and we still have to this day. She
is like a daughter to me. Her name is Pat Todd. Well, on
the second visit to Jersey, which became a regular thing,
Pat came to all the meetings. In one of the meetings there
was a lady in a wheelchair and I felt that I needed some
oil to anoint her with before I prayed. There was none
in the church, so Pat said there was a shop down the
road, she would fetch some. The shop was closed due to
bereavement. Pat thought "what now?" She said the Holy
Spirit led her to a public house to get the oil. When she
got to the bar and asked for oil, the barman told her they
only sell alcohol and not oil. The guy thought she was a
bit strange and called the manager, and then Pat explained
what it was all about. He said he could help.

The manager goes upstairs and descends with a large
bottle of cooking oil, hands it to Pat and tells her she can
keep it, also mentioning that his sister was in a wheelchair
and was going to such a meeting. Pat arrives with the oil
and shouts that she had the oil but she could only get pub
oil, to which everyone laughed, so we prayed over the pub
oil. The amazing thing is the oil was for that manager's
sister. She was raised out of her wheelchair and went

straight to the pub to show her brother. He too got saved and sold the pub. At the closing of the meeting, we had a great time. Two little old ladies came to me and told me that whilst I was talking they wanted the floor to swallow them up. My reply was that they must have been guilty of something. Then to my astonishment they told me they were involved with the treatment we suffered in the home. One was in charge of the beatings with nettles when we wet the bed; the other lady was in charge of the ice cold baths of water. My old nature came back as I grabbed them both by the neck and wanted to beat them up. Both ladies began to cry. They told me they would understand if there was no forgiveness from me. There was none. I said, "I cannot forgive you. As I look at you I can recall the pain".

So we stood for a while bearing in mind the church was still full of people who did not understand what was going on. At that point God spoke to me and said, "if you cannot forgive them, how can I forgive you?" Thinking that was a bit harsh, the beatings we had were real, my reply was, "well you never had what we had". "No I did not," was God`s reply, "but my Son did when He went to the Cross of Calvary, He suffered more than you ever have or ever will." With that I dropped on my knees and cried to God to forgive me for what I was going to do to those ladies, then standing up and facing them gave them a big hug and forgave them, then had the joy of leading them to the Lord and praying with them. They were released from guilt, so was I. You may be thinking, why did I need to forgive them, as they were the ones who were cruel, not you? The Bible says in Ephesians 4 verse 32, "be kind and compassionate to one another, forgiving each other, just as Christ in God forgave you." To hold unforgiveness and hatred eats at you like a cancer and you are the one that suffers in the long run. I had felt angry and bitter towards those people for many years. Now that pent up feeling has gone.

On one visit to Jersey it was to be a holiday and to rest. The RE teacher asked me to speak at one of his classes, so it was agreed I would do the Monday morning. The other children were so jealous that the headmaster asked if I would talk to all the children and the teachers, as he felt it was unfair for some to hear my story and not the others. Some days there were two classes in one room, some sitting on the cupboards or wherever they could. The headmaster told me that he had never seen the children so keen to listen to me. In fact the headmaster himself came one morning to hear me. He gave me a free hand to pray with the children. The result was some of them gave their lives to Jesus. One girl told me she had very bad epilepsy and was unable to use a computer. She asked for prayer. Two days later she told me she had not had a fit since the prayer. Normally she had one at least once a day, and she had been able to use the computer with no trouble at all. When I visit Jersey now, at the headmaster's request, I can visit the children in his school.

France was an experience I shall never forget. There have been many visits. All have funny stories and great meetings. One family that hosted me were an elderly couple. The house was more like a big castle where the meetings were held. The day had been very tiring and I was ready for my bed. The lady of the house showed me to the bedroom which had a large four poster bed. On the pillow was a white frilly nightdress and a Wee Willy Winkie hat. I explained that I had my own nightwear but she insisted it was a gift. Not to seem ungrateful I put the nightdress on, plus the hat, then was ready to get onto to the bed. I could not get on it because the bed was too high to start with, but also the covers were silk material so there was nowhere to grip. So the next idea was to stand by the wall then run and jump on the bed. The problem was I went clean over the other side and onto the floor. The lady came into my room as she heard the bang from me landing on the floor, then she got me a chair to climb on the bed, laughing. As I looked in the mirror and saw what I looked like, the hat came off as soon as she left the room. Next morning on the way to the bathroom, there was the master of the house wearing his nightwear and his hat. Trying to keep a straight face was hard.

11 *Meeting the Royal Family*

This is a day I will never forget. I had an early flight in the morning to minister at a disabled centre in Toulouse. On arrival I noticed a West Indian lady in a wheelchair then I saw a picture of her getting out of her wheelchair and walking. As I shared this with the lady who travelled with me, she told me if that happened it would certainly be a miracle. She was 20 years of age and was born with a deformity and had never walked, let alone stand. My heart went out to these people as they lived in that complex to be looked after. We started the meeting. I shared my story, then showed the video, which they watched with anticipation, clapping and cheering all the time it was being shown. The first lady to be prayed for was West Indian and in a wheelchair. She was born with a chronic deformity and had never been able to stand or walk.

This lady was 20 years of age and very beautiful. As I prayed for her tears welled up in my eyes as I thought of the night I was in the same situation. This lady gradually started to come out of her wheelchair and stood up with a little help from the carers, and then she told them to leave her alone as she was going to be healed and walk for the first time. As I continued to pray her legs seemed to become stronger and she was walking on her own, then she began to do a sprint. She had received her miracle. The reality is that once she was healed she was no longer allowed to stay in that home. She had to find other accommodation, which I am sure she was more than happy to do. This lifted people's faith. As a gentleman came for prayer, I noticed his legs were a funny shape. He told me he had never been able to wear long trousers. As a result, as he received prayer, one of the carers started to cry and shouted to me that his legs were completely straight. He then shouted to her to fetch him a pair of long trousers to put on. He too had to leave those premises and find another place to live. This certainly was a testimony to the proof of their miracles.

I flew back to Paris where my two friends were waiting for me, and expressed all I wanted to do was to soak in a nice warm bath and put my feet up. They laughed and said, "you can have a bath, then you are going to meet some of the royal family. You are invited to the banquet tonight as a guest". Looking at them I said there is no way I wanted to go, as I did not speak fluent French. In any case they did not know me and would not miss me. Also I had no dress with me fit for a banquet, and that was a way out until my friend told me that God had told them what dress to buy me and also the colour. Praying that it would not fit me, God ignored that prayer. The dress and colour were perfect. They informed me it was Prince Charles and Princess Diana that the banquet was for, as they had come to unveil a plaque. The time came to be introduced to Prince Charles and then to Princess Diana. She looked beautiful and was very charming.

Prince Charles started to engage in conversation, asking me what I was doing in France and I obliged by telling him the reason for the visit and giving him a little of my story and told him about the visit to Toulouse. He wanted to know what denomination I belonged to, so told him Assemblies of God and in his deep voice he informed me he knew it was like the Elim movement where they preach people were sinners. At this point I forgot who I was talking to and said, "well you are", and quoted John 3 verse 16, "For all have sinned and come short of the glory of God". There was no point in leaving him in thin air and I also told them both it did not exempt the royal family. He went on to ask me how I performed as I pray for the sick. My reply was the Lord guides me what to do. Then he wanted me to demonstrate as if he were blind, which obviously was a bit risky, as he was heavily guarded by the French police.

The next part of the conversation was to ask if I had ever been to London and seen Buckingham Palace. My answer was that I had only stood outside of the gates but that it was a beautiful building, and then suggested that I also have a Palace waiting for me to go to when I died. It is called Heaven. By this time he was ready to unveil the plaque. Then we went into this massive hall where the table was set out with our names and I sat three places from Princess Diana.

The latest visit to France was very recently, to Brittany. Caroline Barrow, who God sent to minister with me, is also my prayer partner as we travel around. We flew to Dinard. When we got to the airport we could not believe how small the airport was. We were through customs, got the luggage and out of the building in less than twenty minutes. We were met by my friend Angela Walters. This was an emotional time as Angela's husband David, who was a pastor, had recently passed away, so I was there on a double mission, one to be with Angela and pay my respects to David who was a very good friend to both John and myself over the years, the other was to minister to the people. My friend Pat from Jersey had also come to pay her respects to David.

Aymeric Bimont arranged the first meeting in Le Moustoir church where his father was Pastor. We had an evening service. People listened to my story, and then the DVD of my miracle was shown. The enemy tried to disrupt the meeting, but we know God is in control. People responded to come and get prayer. They were not disappointed as the power of God was working in people's lives. The Pastor came for prayer. He had been experiencing chronic stomach pain for some time every day. Aymeric told me from that night his father had been completely healed. The pain had completely gone. Another lady said she had trouble with her spine. All the pain had gone. On Sunday I spoke on forgiveness and what a relief it brings when you put grudges aside and forgive. I also shared healings and miracles that I had seen on my travels. Caroline and I prayed for people and the Holy Spirit moved in power, then we had a fellowship lunch together in the church, then had a wonderful time in praise and worship, then after a long day went back home for tea and a rest. There was a house group on the Monday afternoon. I asked Caroline to speak at that. Pat went home that day. Caroline and I travelled home the following day. I would like at this point to say a big thank you to Caroline's husband Chris, who releases his wife from a busy schedule to travel with me. They own a public house called The Flying Ferret in Huddersfield. This is no ordinary public house. It is run on Christian principles with no bad language or drugs and the people are all very friendly and seem to help each other. They hold Christian activities very often and when I visit them there are people waiting to chat with me and have needs for healing. We hope to visit Brittany again next year.

I was invited to speak at a tent crusade with John Wimber in Paris. On the last morning of the crusade I shared with him a sort of dream that I had in the night. I saw a group of people trying to sort a bill out and getting very frustrated as there was not enough money to pay the bill. Then I saw a great tent, then realised that the bill was something to do with the crusade. As I woke up thinking, "Lord, what is the meaning of this dream?", the answer was that in the morning service there was to be a silent offering as the coins were not enough to pay the deficit that was owed to pay the bill and were God's people prepared to let this happen? John told me to give this out and ask for the offering. The £2,000 pounds came in the offering to pay the bill, plus extra money towards another crusade. John told me to go and pray for a Jamaican lady who had trouble with her jaw. As I was praying for her she went onto the floor of the tent and reacted like a snake. Not seeing this before, I called for John. He just shouted to me "just speak in tongues, sister". The sweat was pouring down my face. As I prayed that lady was completely set free. She had dabbled with snakes and witchcraft.

12 *The Emerald Isle*

John and I had many visits to Ireland, travelling from the North to the South and East to West. There are too many places to mention that we have visited. The place is full of beauty and we came to love the people. There were different things that impressed us, one of them being the respect at a funeral as the hearse went down the street past the shops and houses, and the respect people showed for each another. To mention a few places that we visited, Dublin, Donegal, Waterford, where the crystal glassware is made, Cork, Galway, Larne, Armagh, Tipperary, Lisburn and Sligo, Brookborough, these are but a few. The Pastor in Brookborough was Paul Dunn and his wife Iris. I have stayed in their home on many occasions and loved to listen to him playing his guitar singing the old Gospel songs.

On one occasion they picked me up from the airport and on the way to their house Paul took a wrong turning. There was a hush in the car, which I thought was strange. I sat in the back with his son. Paul made a remark he would not normally take that route, not even in the daylight. Blow me if he made the same mistake again. He explained we were in Crossmaglen, which was notorious for snipers jumping out from the hedges and stopping the driver of the car, pointing a gun at him, ordering him and his passengers out of the car. I was told if that happened, just to get out of the car and not to speak. I had no idea he meant the IRA. Eventually he found the right route home with great relief that was felt by all.

I recall on one Sunday night there were so many people that came out to the front for ministry; Paul said his fingers were sore from playing the guitar. A very special lady to me, named Iona, heard I was speaking at the church and would be praying for the sick. She decided to come along on the Sunday evening when the sick were being prayed for. She felt led to stand in proxy for a lady called Margaret who had been in a coma for five days and was on a life support machine. The family had been told the machine would be turned off on the Monday to see if she could manage on her own. I asked the church to stand with us in prayer for Margaret asking God that when the machine was turned off she would be able to amaze the doctors. Monday morning the family gathered for a meeting with the doctors. Their verdict was not good news, as they told them that she really was brain dead and did not give them any hope. If she lived she would be like a cabbage. The moment came for the machine to be turned off and the doctors could not believe the response as Margaret's daughter said, "mum, open your eyes." Margaret opened her eyes and smiled. She was restored to full health and was able to be discharged two weeks later. Margaret is still well as I write this book and living life to the full.

Iona took a prayer cloth to a man whose liver was decaying. The doctors were talking about a liver transplant. He was in a serious condition, also in a lot of discomfort and pain. His name was Roy and his wife was Lila. I prayed over a prayer cloth, praying that God would burn the sickness out from his body and give him new kidneys. The instructions were put down on paper for him to put the cloth on his back or front by his kidneys, which he did. When after a while he called to his wife to check his back, he was sure she would find blisters. She assured him his skin was not even red. Roy was healed completely. Lila and Roy both say it was his life saver. Both of them gave their hearts to Jesus and are members of that church. People begin to believe for healing when they see or have proof of something definitely happening. Iona is a very special lady. Her ministry is providing me with prayer cloths, also often sending me requests to pray over these cloths for her friends. A big thank you, Iona. This has been very special to me and these prayer cloths have been sent all over the world.

A ladies' coffee morning was one I shall never forget. A lady was brought to the meeting by her daughters. She looked so ill and could hardly stand on her feet. She was so weak. Her daughters told me she was 94 years of age, had ovarian cancer, and only had three days to live. My thoughts were she would be better off in bed but her daughters had been praying she would get saved before she died. By this time I had told the Pastor and my husband John to go and have a game of pool or darts somewhere as this was a ladies' meeting, so off they went for a couple of hours. We had a time of praise and worship. The lady called to me and told me she was uncomfortable sitting on the hard chair. The Pastor's wife suggested we lay her on the settee that was at the back of the church. She would still be able to hear what I was saying. As she lay down, she said she only had three days to live, but she was not going to last that long. She was going now. My reaction was that it was a healing meeting and people cannot die in a healing meeting. The inevitable happened as she groaned and took her last breath.

The Pastor's wife, who was a nursing sister, checked her pulse and confirmed she could not find one. The question was what to do, so I suggested we turn the chairs round and I would stand in front of the settee as she had gone to sleep. I was not lying. Really, she was just sleeping deeper than I wanted her to sleep. Then something strange happened. The Holy Spirit spoke so clearly to me and said, "has it not been spoken over you, my child, that you will see the dead raised?" I swallowed hard. I thought, I am not ready for this. That is for the big preachers like Reinhard Bonnke and Benny Hinn. Then I felt two hands turn me around to face the lady. I started to break the spirit of death and called to God to burn the cancer to the roots and give her back her life, then turned to carry on speaking. There was such a shout of elation when the lady stood up behind me with her hands in the air and gave her life to Jesus.

She went for a meal with her family and ate a four course meal, bearing in mind she had not eaten for four days, only taking sips of water. The following day John and I visited her bungalow to have a wee lunch with her, and she was trying to teach me to do Irish dancing. That miracle never happened. The Lord gave her three more months to live and prompted her to gather friends and neighbours in to hear her story. This she did and 15 people became Christians that day, then she told them Jesus was taking her home to heaven that night and not to get me to pray her back this time as she was ready to go to heaven. She went that night.

Visiting Madras in India a few times has a special place in my heart. As I have visited children's homes who have been orphaned, it brings back memories of my own childhood. Pastor John Rajah is a man of God who has such a heart for such children and has seen the homes being opened, the children being looked after by volunteers, also seeing they have a Christian upbringing and a good education. I have worked with Pastor John, not only with the children, but spreading the Gospel and preaching the Word of God. At one open air meeting where I preached, when the time came to pray for the sick, the people just flocked in their hundreds to be prayed for. The only problem is when they have been prayed for they go to the back of the queue and come for more prayer. At one open air meeting a mother came forward for prayer cradling a small child. The child was covered in black sores. I asked Pastor John to ask her what the sores were. He told me it was a type of leprosy. My reaction was that if I touch the child it could be contagious. On the other hand the thought that came to me was if Jesus was standing here instead of me, He would take the child in His arms and pray for the child to be healed. At that moment I took the child from the mother, put some oil on the child's head, and prayed for her to be healed. Two nights later at another crusade this lady came on the platform and in her arms was this beautiful little girl. She was the same child that had the leprosy. There was not a mark or scar on her body. She had been healed to the glory of God.

At a Pastors' and their wives' conference, where the hall was packed to capacity, people had travelled from different parts of India. I preached on the woman with the issue of blood from Mark 5 verses 24 to 34. The time came to pray for people. In India the men sit apart from the women and a man prays for the men and a lady prays for the women. As I was going to pray for one of the ladies she began to cry. She told me that she suffered with the same complaint as the woman in the Bible for a long period of time and could not afford the doctor's fees. She also had said to her husband if the preacher mentions that story she would be healed. How amazing. That is exactly what I preached on. She had prayer and soon after she testified that the bleeding had stopped.

One small church I was asked to speak at on the Sunday morning was way out in the bush area. As the people were coming into the church a man came in wearing warrior attire, holding a spear in his hand. I was informed to be on my guard as he had never been at the church before. He obviously was from the bush area. I gave my story of my miracle, then made an appeal for people to give their lives to Jesus. When this man raced to the front of the church pointing the spear at me, my thought was, is this the way I am going to die? But as he got near to me he fell on his knees calling out, "I can't do it". He had been sent to kill me. Instead he gave his life to Jesus. That man got rid of all the fetishes that he was wearing and became a member of that church. God knew I was not to die that day.

A visit to Germany for some more meetings with Pastor Reinhard Bonnke and the team. One of the meetings was in a field. It was a very cold, wet night and Reinhard preached the Gospel. People listened and responded to the call of salvation. As we were praying with people, I was told to pray for a lady who was wearing a long black raincoat. As I began to pray, the Lord showed me a large knife inside a pocket in her coat, so asking her about it was shocked to hear her story. The lady told me she had been walking around the outside of the field. In fact she had walked around nine times. On the tenth time she was drawn into the field to the meeting and got saved. She had contemplated killing her husband and cutting up his body before disposing of him. She confessed to her husband and told him everything. He came to the meeting the following night and gave his life to Jesus as well. Before I flew home I had the privilege of having lunch at Reinhard's home, before having a guided tour to see the CFAN head offices in Frankfurt. I recall at the lunch Reinhard giving me a word from God that I would travel to many places and that I would see many things happen in the ministry and that has happened, but he did not know that the same word had been given to me by to other people. We said goodbye and then I was driven to the airport for the journey home.

I am very fond of Holland and have visited many times to different churches. Staying in Hilversum with Pastor Teun and his wife Tessa De Ruiter with John, these people became very good friends of ours and still are. At the first meeting there was a lady who came for prayer. She was a hostess on the airline. She contracted HIV, and was told she may lose her job. She came to the front. I prayed against the HIV. Three weeks later she was at the hospital for a check-up, and to her joy the tests were clear. She was back at work the following week. In the same meeting there was another lady sitting near the wall. She had felt led to bring her son Andrew's baby vest for me to pray over it as Andrew was in a special care unit in hospital not expected to live many days. The vest was anointed with oil and taken to the hospital where Andrew lay in an incubator. Within days the doctors were amazed at the improvement that Andrew was making. This was a great trial for his mother and two older brothers and sister but she never gave up the hope of having him home. His mother is like a daughter to me. Her name is Sita. We have come to love each other and I have stayed in her home and met Andrew who is such a loving child. He still needs special care in some ways, but he calls me Nanny Jean and speaks on the phone to me. Andrew plays football and loves to play the game. God is a miracle working God and still heals today, which amazes the doctors when they do not have the answers themselves. Luke was a doctor in the Bible.

Blind eyes have been opened at such meetings and deaf ears opened. The dumb speak and the lame walk. I have seen these miracles with my own eyes. A lady who had lost the will to laugh and be happy, as all her family had been killed in a minibus accident, after prayer was released and set free and was able to laugh again for the first time in six months and was able to start looking to the future. Tern and Tessa also became very good friends of ours and when we stayed in their home we had such happy times together. We would laugh as after a meal John would put on his yellow marigold gloves and got stuck into doing the dishes. He did this in many homes that we stayed in. He enjoyed doing it. A big thank you, Tern, for your teaching into my ministry over the years and Sita for your love and friendship over all these years. May God bless you. I also ministered over the years in the church where Sita worshipped and had some very powerful meetings as God moved in people's lives. Her pastor was Hendrick Young. I have happy memories of being there at their special Christmas that they celebrate, called Black Pete, with dancing in the street so they have two Christmases to celebrate.

I have been to Portugal. I was doing ground promotion preparation for Reinhard before a Fire Conference. The meeting took place in this large hall. The place was packed with people with expectation of what was going to happen. The Lord gave me the figure 50. This kept going through my head. Standing by the wall were a crowd of young people smoking and drinking cans of alcohol. I beckoned to the pastor and told him I was going to ask them to take their cigarettes and cans of alcohol outside and they could fetch them after the meeting. He advised me that the previous night the preacher asked them to do the same and they threw their cans at him. I asked if I could have a carrier bag with a few empty cans on the platform. I faced the group and reminded them of what they did the night previously and asked who was going to throw the first can, as I had three in my hand as a dare. But they took their drink and cigarettes outside, then came back in. 50 young people gave their lives to Jesus; among them were the ones that stood by the wall.

The time had come to pray for the sick. There was no room at the front of the stage so I called them onto the platform. The first to be prayed for was a young lad who asked me to pray for his smoking addiction. As I was about to pray I had a picture of a packet of cigarettes with the word drugs on it. The person praying with me had the same picture, so I explained what I had been shown. He said, "I suppose Him up there showed you that", and pointed to the ceiling. I prayed that the next cigarette he smoked would taste nasty and make him sick. He remarked that it was not a nice prayer. This lad had got a black patch over his left eye. He lifted the patch from off his eye and I noticed that the eye socket was empty. He challenged me to see what my God could do to give him a new eye. At that moment I was led to call another young lad who was wearing a bright yellow sweater to come onto the platform. This lad was in a fight with the lad I was praying for. He lost his eye because he was about to stab the other lad. He fell and the knife went into his eye.

I must admit this was a bit of a challenge being on the platform. I put my hands over his eye and his head shook from side to side. He pulled my hands down and said it felt like fire coming from my hands. I told him that I would just pray. He confirmed it was alright to put my hands back on his eyes when his head shook from side to side again, and as he pulled my hands away for the second time, with witnesses watching, an eye dropped into the empty socket and he could see. Also it was the same colour as the other eye. This lad was in shock so he went outside and lit up a cigarette and was violently sick. As I went outside to check him after his friends called me, he said "it does not matter. God has answered your first prayer as well". That young lad settled in a church in the area and the two lads who once were enemies became good friends.

13 *Visit to Finland*

This is a report back from Pastor Pasi Turunen from Patmos Foundation for World Missions in Finland that he printed after the visit. He writes, "Glory to Jesus, we were prepared for some healing miracles, but God who always exceeds our expectations gives us more than we ask. We had a few intense spiritual charged ministry days with Jean in Finland, April 2011. She is a walking miracle, or a running miracle, to be precise. I met her at the airport. I thought I would be greeted by an old and frail British lady. I was so wrong. She outran me not only at the airport but wherever we went with her.

Meetings were arranged in three major cities in Finland, Helsinki, which is the capital city, Turku and Tampere. In each city we had a capacity crowd. In some places we had to fetch more chairs to accommodate the people. Hundreds of people filled the churches and halls. People burst into spontaneous applause as they heard Jean's awesome testimony and were shouting praises to God as they saw her running up and down the aisles like a young girl. Usually it is hard to get a single AMEN from the audience. Believe me, I should know. In each city, together with her friend Caroline, she ministered patiently as countless people lined up to be prayed for. My back and feet ached but she kept on going until the last person in the room was prayed for, ready to run again. It is as if Isaiah had her in mind when he wrote the words in Isaiah 40 verse 30-31.

People had heard Jean in our nationwide radio broadcast tell about the miracles God had performed through her ministry all over the world, and God did not disappoint us either. The atmosphere in each city was charged with the power of the Holy Spirit. There was expectation in the air. Everywhere people were touched by the power of the Holy Spirit. There were both physical and spiritual healings. For example, months later as I was preaching in Saint Michael's Church, a lady came and gave me a note that read, "I want to give glory to the Lord. At the meeting in Saint Michael's in Turku in April, an English lady prayed for me and my neck was healed. I do not need any further chiropractic treatment. Praise God".

The night she landed we had a youth meeting. She was teaching about receiving and retaining healing, and the importance of forgiveness in receiving your miracle. That message was extremely important. She went on to challenge the people to live out their Christian faith in practical ministry towards those who are hurting and lonely. Jean's message was a much needed timely message of hope. She was led by the Spirit to open her life before the Finnish audience the way she did. Her testimony did not fall on deaf ears nor leave hearts untouched. Many people came to me later on how deeply affected and encouraged they were by her testimony. I had the opportunity to pray with some later on and see their tears as God was using her testimony to mend their broken hearts. Her visit to Finland left a lasting impact to many lives; her testimony and ministry brought healing and hope to many people."

This is a report from Pastor Oliver Raper Senior on my first visit to South Africa, which I take it a privilege to put in this the book. "On one of our overseas ministry trips in 1988, after we had been visiting our family at CFAN headquarters, quite casually we heard about this remarkable healing that had taken place earlier that year. It was our privilege on arrival to Birmingham to be Reinhard Bonnke's guest at the Fire Conference where we found ourselves seated in the VIP area and I began to wish and pray that I could meet this woman that had been healed. To my delight Jean Neil, the person concerned, came to where we were seated and although we were total strangers, she took the seat next to me. This gave me the opportunity I was looking for.

After we had heard of this miraculous healing from the person concerned, I took the liberty of inviting her to South Africa on a Tour of Witness, so early in 1989 we welcomed her at Johannesburg Airport and began the "Tour of Witness". Jean had difficulty in expressing herself adequately at first. It soon became my task of guiding her testimony along the most effective lines. We visited Maranatha Park Conference where a few thousand people were privileged to hear her story. To shouts of approval and clapping of hands, Jean then ran around this great crowd in record time.

In Cape Town we experienced a critical comment from a medical doctor whose religious views made him discredit any miraculous healing. Valiantly Jean continued with her simple straightforward report. In Cape Town there was a large gathering in Goodwood who would rejoice at the report of the power of God in evidence today. Slowly the habit grew for her to call us Mom and Dad and over the years she came to see herself as an adopted daughter and part of our family, much to our delight. A wonderful bond of love and friendship has grown out of her ministry trips together.

In Port Elizabeth she gave her testimony to a crowded Feather Market Hall and when I said to her, "Jean will you run and demonstrate your healing?" a boy of about ten years of age decided to run with her to the merriment of the crowd. He could not keep up with this speedy flight of testimony. As more and more detail came into this report she was giving, my own faith took flight. While we were in Southern Cape, we took her to an ostrich farm. There was a noticeboard saying for a small price you could ride an ostrich. Jean began to pester me to be given the fun of such a ride. I remonstrated with her, bearing in mind that she was no youngster herself, and, after all, it was not very comely for a woman to be riding an ostrich. My objections were dashed aside and this once occupant of a wheelchair, after being set free of 25 years of suffering, put her arms around the big bird's neck and as it raced along I don't know whose mouth was open the widest, Jeans or the ostrich's. What a delight to see the extent of God's healing power.

Another highlight was in Natal where her testimony was given to a crowded hall in Pietermaritsburg. A medical doctor who was in the service and I invited him to examine Jean and give us his comments. Needless to say she passed with flying colours. I was greatly gratified to notice how her ability to express herself grew clearer and stronger with every visit. When eventually the time came to say goodbye we took her to a farm to the north of Pretoria where Ria and I joined her in a very rough ride in a cross country vehicle rented for the occasion. When it was over she was laughing hilariously and we were complaining about the extreme discomfort we had to put up with.

This then is the picture we retain. Recently she visited Southern Cape in George area and it was wonderful to see the healings taking place in response to the testimonies of God's goodness. We count it a privilege to have taken this testimony of the Lord's faithfulness in healing to a large number of people here in the Southern tip of Africa and to be able to report that when faith had achieved its purpose we witnessed healing upon healings everywhere. Our prayer remains for Jean to go forth as a continued witness to awaken the truth of Divine Healing".

14 *Dedicated to My Husband, John*

I have written this book in memory of John who was over 50 years my husband, soul mate, father to my four children, grandfather to my grandchildren and great granddad to my great grandchildren. I thank God that we had so many happy years together. Yes, we had our differences but we worked through the difficult times. Thank you, Lord. You gave me a husband who cared for us all and took his marriage vows seriously and stood by their principles till the day he passed away. Thank you for all the years you helped me bear my sickness and tenderly looked after me until that day I received my miracle, and even that night you were by my side, then the time came for me to look after you through your time of illness which you had for eight years. The nine weeks you lay in hospital unconscious after the stroke, I thought I had lost you then, but God knew it was not your time yet.

When we took our marriage vows in 1958 they were for real, they were for better or worse, in sickness and in health, till death us do part, and that is what we did and that is what marriage is, about learning to understand each other and forgiving each other when we make mistakes, trying never to hate each other or hold a grudge. God forgave us when He gave His Son on the Cross of Calvary.

That is why forgiveness is a big part of our healing. It gets rid of all the anger and bitterness.

My heart was broken when you had to go into care and God knew the right place for you to be looked after. The walks to and from the care home kept me fit. You were a little tinker at times when you played them up, but you also gave a lot of joy and laughter. Then the real blow came, being told you had cancer. The last few weeks of our lives together were extra special in Willow Tree Nursing Home, sleeping by your side, knowing each day was nearer to losing you, but even then you bore your pain till the end without a grudge and even witnessed about Heaven and Hell. The morning you shut your eyes for the last time my heart was ripped apart. I know that we will meet again with full assurance. We all miss you very much. Again, a big thank you for being part of my life and the family. Till we meet again, God bless you.

I would like to say a big thank you to all the people that have been there for us in the past to guide us to do the right things and to walk the way God wants us to walk. I want to say a big thank you to two very special people in Rugby Assist office, Barbara who helped me through some of the traumatic times of my childhood, and Julie who has helped me through the trauma of losing John and the recent new findings about my parents. A big thank you to you both. At these times they have been very helpful. You are two very special people. This service is there to help anyone who is going through trauma or a difficult time, I have been extremely glad of their help and guidance. To the staff at Dewar Close who nursed John for eight years with great patience and in the last week of his life the caring staff at the Willow Tree Nursing Home. To Doctor West and Doctor Leach, who helped right through to the end. Pastors Val and Lily Cunningham, Pastor David and

Sheila Crabb and my Pastor Barry Killick and his wife Susan, also Pastor John Macdonald, Reinhard and the whole team from Christ for All Nations. Last, but not least, I want to say a big thank you to my children, also my sister Roselle who has done so much for me. Also William Dallow and his wife Amanda who set up my website for me and have given me so much help since I have known them. The person I want to thank the most is Jesus, who went to the Cross for my sins and my sickness, I am where I am today because He has changed my life so much.

If this book has helped you come to terms with similar things that I have experienced then I give God the glory but if you are still struggling with issues then there is a Light at the end of the tunnel and His name is Jesus.